The OFFICIAL
Print Shop
Handbook

The OFFICIAL
Print Shop
Handbook

IDEAS, TIPS, AND DESIGNS FOR HOME, SCHOOL AND PROFESSIONAL USE

Randi Benton and Mary Schenck Balcer

Foreword by Doug Carlston, President of Broderbund Software

BANTAM BOOKS
TORONTO · NEW YORK · LONDON · SYDNEY · AUCKLAND

THE OFFICIAL PRINT SHOP HANDBOOK: TIPS, AND DESIGNS FOR HOME,
SCHOOL, AND PROFESSIONAL USE

THE OFFICIAL PRINT SHOP HANDBOOK
A Bantam Book/December 1987

ISBN O-553-34453-6

Published simultaneously in the United States and Canada

Bantam Books are published by Bantam Books, Inc. Its trademark, consisting of the words ''Bantam Books'' and the por-
trayal of a rooster, is Registered in U.S. Patent and Trademark
Office and in other countries. Marca Registrada. Bantam Books,
Inc., 666 Fifth Avenue, New York, New York 10103.

PRINTED IN THE UNITED STATES OF AMERICA

0 9 8 7 6 5 4 3 2 1

Contents

New and Modified Art

Planning Tools

Foreword

By Doug Carlston

When David Balsam and Marty Kahn first showed us an early version of a program later to be called The Print Shop, we were struck with the extraordinary creativity it permitted even the most artistically hopeless of us. However, we never suspected that The Print Shop would become one of the precursors to a whole new category of software applications referred to as desktop publishing. Nor did we anticipate the breadth of original and creative publishing uses The Print Shop users would find for the product once they got their hands on it.

Users have sent thousands of letters describing how they used The Print Shop to create everything from a stencil for painting the name on a sailboat, to a world-record-setting 1.7 mile long banner. They have used The Print Shop to make gift wrapping, Christmas ornaments, party hats and to frame pictures. In short, they have shown us a wealth of ideas for the use of The Print Shop that goes far beyond what we had originally conceived of ourselves. That is the reason why this book was written. It is designed to expand the user's vision of what he can do with The Print Shop and to encourage the sharing of ideas, tools, guides, hints and design techniques.

We have expanded the potential of the original Print Shop with companion products such as The Print Shop Graphic Libraries. Many of the graphic images we developed were initiated by the unique and unusual art sent us by users of The Print Shop. We were therefore very pleased when Randi Benton and Mary Balcer told us of their intention to compile a handbook on The Print Shop which would bring together some of the best tips and techniques into a single reference work.

I am delighted to see this work come into being and hope that it helps you get the most out of The Print Shop. If we can each benefit a little from the inspirations of others, we all end up that much more creative; a fact evidenced by the evolution of The Print Shop.

Authors' Notes

While vacationing in the south of France last fall, my husband and I spent some of our most enjoyable evenings in the tiny hilltown of Mougins. There are no streets to speak of in this medieval, cobble-stoned village, only narrow, winding lanes. Yet here one finds more than a fair representation of magnificent views, gourmet restaurants, and art. Hanging from restored houses and storefronts are signs carved in stone, sculpted in iron. Everything about Mougins suggests an appreciation of beauty—an artful lifestyle.

It was here that we visited the Musée de Mougins, a tiny museum housed in an old stone building with a pond in its center. And in this most unlikely environment we came across the business cards of a local artist on exhibit—created by The Print Shop! The flyers promoting the exhibit were created by The Print Shop, too! The Print Shop had found its way to this tiny hilltown of France!

Shortly after we returned home, the impact of The Print Shop hit again. It was early October, better known as baseball playoff season in our family. During Game 4 of the American League playoffs the cameras zeroed in on an oversized sign in the stands that read:

ROSES ARE RED
VIOLETS ARE BLUE
THE ANGELS IN FIVE
I GOT SERIES TICKETS TOO!

I spotted it right away. The sign was created from four Print Shop banners stacked one on top of the other.

Clever ideas. Whether it's the business cards of a French artist or the oversized sign of a California fan, clever ideas for The Print Shop abound. That's why we've created this handbook.

This book is a collection of ideas. Included are the ideas of people who created The Print Shop program. And the ideas of users like yourself. But largely this is a book of ideas that surfaced after Mary and I booted up our Print Shop disks, created our first designs, and then asked ourselves "What next?"

With our collective experience in graphic design, software design, and educational/game design, we set out not only to stretch The Print Shop beyond the obvious but also to shed new light on how to work with the obvious.

We hope you'll keep this book handy when you're thinking about a new Print Shop design. We invite you to copy our ideas. Adapt them. Edit them. Embellish them.

Creative thinking is contagious–you're sure to discover new ideas of your own!

RB

*With special gratitude to my husband Mark–for your patience and perspective–and for planning another visit to Mougins!
Thanks to Kenzi at Bantam, and Ann at Broderbund,
for your help and support.*

*   *   *

For over ten years I have developed personal computer software–and in that relatively short time I have seen the machine that started out as "a solution in search of a need" become an integral tool in the home, in the school, and in business.

The goal of a dedicated computer software developer has always been to best marry the software and the machine in order to make the machine "invisible" and the software then an extension of the user. With its simplicity, coupled with its diversity, The Print Shop accomplishes this goal. It allows students, families, and business people to easily create personalized printed communications that are varied in design and application–thus its empowering quality and success.

We have just scratched the surface with a sample of layouts of applications familiar to the Print Shop users. And the new applications we have considered will, hopefully, only serve to spur your imagination. I hope you enjoy *living* with The Print Shop as much as we (me, Randi, my husband, my daughter, my friends, my helpers) did!

MSB

Thanks to Gary Schenck for doing some very clever designs when I ran out of time and he had none to spare.

Special thanks to Collette Michaud for her infinite patience printing, inputting pixels, trying to figure out how the designs were done — looking at templates, measuring, re-printing, and keeping me in a good mood.

And infinite appreciation to Rob Balcer for contributing organizational ability and moral support, digging in to do whatever was necessary to make our deadlines — and donating all our tables for printers and computers.

About The Handbook

- WHY A HANDBOOK OF IDEAS

- WHAT'S IN THIS BOOK

- HOW TO USE THIS BOOK

- HANDBOOK SYMBOLS – AT A GLANCE

- LET'S GET STARTED

- A FINAL WORD...

Why a Handbook of Ideas

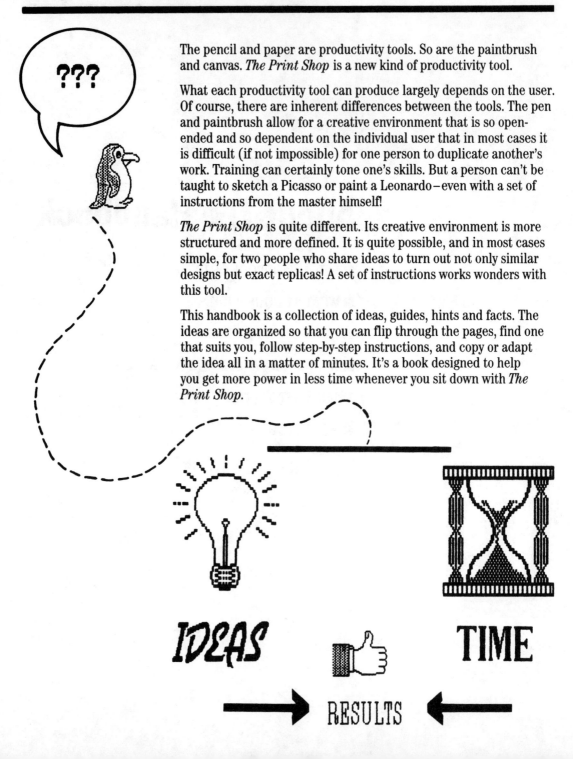

The pencil and paper are productivity tools. So are the paintbrush and canvas. *The Print Shop* is a new kind of productivity tool.

What each productivity tool can produce largely depends on the user. Of course, there are inherent differences between the tools. The pen and paintbrush allow for a creative environment that is so open-ended and so dependent on the individual user that in most cases it is difficult (if not impossible) for one person to duplicate another's work. Training can certainly tone one's skills. But a person can't be taught to sketch a Picasso or paint a Leonardo – even with a set of instructions from the master himself!

The Print Shop is quite different. Its creative environment is more structured and more defined. It is quite possible, and in most cases simple, for two people who share ideas to turn out not only similar designs but exact replicas! A set of instructions works wonders with this tool.

This handbook is a collection of ideas, guides, hints and facts. The ideas are organized so that you can flip through the pages, find one that suits you, follow step-by-step instructions, and copy or adapt the idea all in a matter of minutes. It's a book designed to help you get more power in less time whenever you sit down with *The Print Shop*.

IDEAS + TIME → RESULTS ←

What's in This Book

As avid Print Shop users we appreciate the ease with which greeting cards, signs, banners and letterheads can be created. But most of us only scratch the surface of what *The Print Shop* can do. In this book are hundreds of ideas to help you get beyond that surface.

Ideas for Home, School and Professional Use

You need an idea for a party announcement. A school or club announcement. A business announcement. You've come to the right place!
The Print Shop is used by so many different people for so many different reasons. Yet, most applications fall into one of five categories: *Home, Party, Learning Materials, School/Organization,* or *Professional,* and that's exactly how the designs in the handbook are organized. In this way, you can get right to the idea that will mostly likely apply to your particular need.

New Ideas for Old Applications

You need a sophisticated looking sign for an office get-together. A playful sign for a child's room. And an attention-getting flyer for a garage sale. Where do you begin? With this book, of course. Included are a large assortment of signs, greeting cards, letterheads and banners with different looks and styles for different purposes. There are ideas to illustrate where, when and how to make the most of a sign—or a banner. Easy-to-copy techniques used by professional designers will even help give your original designs a more polished look.

New Applications

There's no rule that the sign mode can only be used to create signs. The sign mode can be used to make wrapping paper and flyers or to type memos. The sign and letterhead modes can generate great business cards. In this book are designs for more than 25 different kinds of items you can make using the four basic Print Shop modes.

Design Concepts

Designs often illustrate basic design concepts. For example, a design may show how a certain kind of graphic or font can be used to deliver a message. Fundamental design concepts are illustrated and pointed out for you in many of the handbook's designs. These concepts can be applied to your original designs and may even open doors to new ideas.

Two Modes Together or One Mode Twice

Here are two ideas that can really broaden the range of what you can do with *The Print Shop:*

■ Print a design in one mode, roll back your paper to the starting point, and then add text or art using a *different* mode.

■ Print a design in one mode, roll back your paper to the starting point, and then add a second graphic or style of type using the *same* mode.

Use the letterhead and sign modes together, or the sign mode twice. In the chapter Designs, Designs, Designs you'll find many examples.

Modified Print Shop Art

To make a strong graphic statement you may require a solid silhouetted figure or a simple line drawing. Luckily, with *The Print Shop* you may not need to start from scratch! All Print Shop graphics can be easily modified. Included are lots of ideas on how to give Print Shop graphics an entirely new look. There are easy-to-copy techniques to create totally new objects and symbols using existing Print Shop art.

New Art

There are times when even the large assortment of Print Shop graphics just doesn't suit your needs. The New Art section provides easy-to-create alternatives. Each graphic includes suggestions and applications to show you the look or feel each graphic can contribute to a design.

Planning/Time-Saving Devices

A sure way to save time is to plan ahead and know what to expect. Suppose you're about to create a greeting card that calls for a large graphic surrounded by words at the top and bottom. Which graphic and which font size and style should you select? On which lines should you type your message? How many lines can you use and still stay clear of the graphic? The planning section of the handbook eliminates all the guesswork. Easy-to-create tools allow you to see exactly where each graphic and each style and size of type will meet on the page. Now you can fine tune your design before you create it!

Hints and Shortcuts

When you set out to use any software program, talking to someone who's spent time with it almost always reveals a personal list of hints and shortcuts. In preparing this book a number of such lists were consolidated. Many hints and shortcuts appear in this book with the items that utilize them. The most widely applicable ones are also in a separate hint section in Designs, Designs, Designs for you to use and apply to your own designs right away!

How to Use This Book

When you're working with *The Print Shop,* we hope you'll keep this book nearby. We're certain you'll discover many different ways to use the ideas. Here are our suggestions for getting the most mileage out of each section.

The Designs

COPY A DESIGN
When you find a design idea you like, by all means copy it! All designs come with easy-to-follow, step-by-step instructions precisely for that reason.

ADAPT A DESIGN
You find a design idea that would be just right if it only had a few more lines of text. Or a few less lines. Or a different style of type. Or a different graphic. Adapt it! Whenever you're looking for an idea, consider adding to the handbook's ideas. Embellish them. Edit them. Use them as stepping stones to another valuable source of ideas–*you.*

SUBSTITUTE A GRAPHIC
It's been said that a picture is worth a thousand words. Then replacing one picture with another very different one should have dramatic results. It does! When you're looking at a design idea, think about using that same design with the graphic best suited for your message. For many designs, alternative graphics that work well are suggested. But by no means should you restrict yourself to these suggestions. Only you know what will work best for the message you need to convey.

THINK MULTIPURPOSE
For your convenience, the design ideas are organized into five categories: *Home, Party, Learning, Materials, School/Organization, Professional.* However, there may be a letterhead in the professional section that is perfect for your personal use, or a sign in the home section that is perfect for your small business or school. When you're looking for ideas, think multipurpose! Consider designs from all five sections.

COMBINE TWO IDEAS

Many designs in this book are intended to illustrate a single strong concept. For example, some designs demonstrate how and when to use rules with text. Others focus on the selection and placement of graphics. When you're considering a new design idea, think about combining two ideas from the handbook. You may find two ideas (or more) that work extremely well together in one of your own original creations.

USE A DESIGN FOR A DIFFERENT ITEM

You come across a birthday card design that would be perfect for an invitation. Adapt it and use it. You see a greeting card design that would be perfect for a party sign. Even better! Designs for greeting cards and signs, in fact, are interchangeable. The greeting card and sign modes offer the exact same choices for graphics and text. The only difference is that in the sign mode the design prints larger. Therefore, it's easy to apply a greeting card design to a sign and vice versa. Just make the same choices for graphics and text and you're ready to print!

The Art

DON'T FORGET THE OVERVIEW PAGE

When you need a design idea, you may want to start by selecting a graphic element and building from there. The art overview page is a tool to keep in mind. Here you'll find reduced samples of all the new and modified handbook art. It's a great place to start thinking about a look for your design. Finding the right graphic to focus your design may be exactly what's needed for inspiration.

COPY, ADAPT, EMBELLISH

As with the designs, if you find a piece of art you like, you needn't go further. Copy it! But consider adapting the graphics, too. For example, you may want to add more lines or thicker lines to a graphic. You may want to embellish a graphic with a decorative element or even with your initials. You may want to combine parts of two graphics. Or edit and use just part of one graphic. Remember, let the handbook's ideas be your springboard.

MODIFY ANY GRAPHIC

Every Print Shop graphic can be modified. Techniques such as turning Print Shop graphics into silhouette drawings or into black line drawings can be applied to many different items. You can start building your own personal library of graphics.

The Planning Tools

GET TO KNOW THE TEMPLATES...

When you're working on an original Print Shop design, head straight for the templates. These easy-to-create, powerful tools are "design models"–they show where on a page graphics and text will appear. So, for example, if you're thinking about creating a greeting card with small birthday cakes in a staggered pattern and using a small font, just consult the appropriate template. Before you even input the design, you'll know exactly where on the page your graphics and text will appear. You'll see where the two will meet–and where they won't.

We originally created the templates for our personal use in planning the designs for this book. Because they were so helpful to us and our work, we show you how to create them–and use them–for your work. Once you start using the templates, we're certain you'll appreciate how accurately you can predict and control the outcome of your design choices. And like us, you may begin to wonder how you ever lived without them!

GET TO KNOW THE GRAPHICS...

A template shows the graphic in the position you want to use hitting the line of text above it. But to fit your entire message, you need to use that line. Don't panic! And don't rework your design just yet!

The templates show how much space the *largest possible graphic* occupies. Of course, many graphics are narrower, others are shorter. This latter information, how short or tall a graphic is, may be the key to your problem–and solution. If the graphic you want to use is just a few lines shorter than the template box, you may clear that line of text. But does it? Head for the Graphics Specification section to find out. Simply find the graphic you want to use. Every graphic from *The Print Shop, Graphics Library 1, Graphics Library 2, Graphics Library 3* and *Holiday Edition* is included in this section and marked for size. You can determine ahead of time exactly how much space your graphic will use.

PLAN, PLAN, PLAN

Planning is the key to any good design. If you flip through a magazine and look at the placement of graphics and text in articles and ads, you'll notice great variety. In some cases, words and pictures overlap. In others, words surround pictures. Words may appear only at the top or bottom of a page. Pictures may appear only at the top or bottom, or in corners. The designs may look very different, but you can be sure they have one thing in common—the placement of their words and pictures was part of a carefully considered plan.

Why not take the same care in planning your Print Shop designs? Use the handbook's tools to decide early in the conception of a design where to place text and graphics on the page. Fine tune your design before you print it. You'll not only get better results, you're sure to save time—and paper!

GRAPHIC PATTERNS—STUDY THE POSSIBILITIES

When considering design ideas, take a look at the possible patterns formed by the placement of graphics as shown in the templates. The variety of pattern possibilities may trigger ideas, and in some instances you can alter the patterns. Remember, in the greeting card and sign modes there's a custom option for small- and medium-sized graphics that lets you individually select the positions you want to use from the *staggered* pattern.

TEXT CHOICES—STUDY THE POSSIBILITIES

You know exactly what font you want to use for a design, but you're not sure whether to select the small or large size. Just look at the templates and then decide. You'll see exactly how each font size fits in a design. You'll see the maximum number of lines you can use and approximately how many letters will fit on each line.

THINK—CREATIVE LAYOUTS

Try some creative layouts. For example, plan a design with all text on the left and graphics on the right. Try alternating lines of graphics with text, or inserting graphics between words on a line. The possibilities are endless—just let the planning tools works for you!

Handbook Symbols—At A Glance

Throughout the handbook design pages and art pages are easy-to-recognize symbols that tell you at a glance where you are and what you need to create each item. Here are the symbols you'll find:

 Home Designs

 Party Designs

 Learning Material Designs

 School/Organizational Designs

 Professional Designs

 New Art

 Modified Print Shop Art

 Scissors are required

 Copying on a copier is recommended

 The Print Shop

 Graphics Library 1

 Graphics Library 2

 Graphics Library 3

 Holiday Edition

 Companion

Let's Get Started

What You Need to Start Creating

You don't need much! If you're a Print Shop owner with an Apple, IBM or Commodore computer (and accompanying manual for first time users), you're ready to start creating hundreds of new designs. The ideas are right here! If, in addition, you own *Graphics Library 1, Graphics Library 2, Graphics Library 3, Holiday Edition,* or the *Companion*—you'll find lots of ideas for these programs, too.

How the Designs Are Organized

The five design sections *(Home, Party, Learning Materials, School/Organization, Professional)* each have a variety of categories such as letterheads, business cards, flyers, ads, greeting cards, banners, and wrapping paper. Categories with a large number of designs include at least one example that requires *only The Print Shop.* Following these examples, wherever appropriate, are designs that require *Graphics Library 1, Graphics Library 2, Graphics Library 3,* the *Holiday Edition* and the *Companion.*

What You Need for Each Design

To let you know immediately if more than the original Print Shop program itself was used to create a design, every design is marked with symbols for one or more of the following products:

> The Print Shop
> Graphics Library 1
> Graphics Library 2
> Graphics Library 3
> Holiday Edition
> Companion

These symbols appear on the preceding page. (The IBM symbol appears next to the Apple and Commodore symbol when it differs from the Apple and Commodore version.)

Consider Every Design—No Matter Which Programs You Own

When you look at a design, one of the first things you'll notice is the symbol(s) indicating which program(s) was used to create that design. If the design calls for *The Print Shop* program only or an additional program that you own, you know you'll be able to copy or adapt the design quickly and easily. But keep this in mind: **when you see a design that uses a program you don't have, don't rule it out!** In most cases, alternative graphic choices are suggested in the design notes at the bottom of the page. One of these suggestions may be suitable for your purpose. It may even work better! And for many designs you're certain to have substitution ideas of your own.

Following the Step-by-Step Instructions

So let's get started! Just pick out a handbook design and follow the step-by-step instructions. You'll be printing in no time. Instructions are included for every design right on the design page. They lead you through the design, one step at a time, every step of the way. Only one item is left out – the guesswork!

A Final Word...

As soon as we began exploring ideas for this book, we were met by our single greatest challenge – to think creatively. As Roger von Oech recommends in his book *A Whack on the Side of the Head:* "To be more creative, just look at the same thing as everyone else and think something different." We set out to look at *The Print Shop* and *think something different*. To our delight (and a real tribute to *The Print Shop's* creators), the more we looked the more we discovered.

We hope you find the ideas in this book useful – and inspiring. We'd like nothing better than for you to pick up on *The Print Shop* discovery road where we left off!

Designs, Designs, Designs

 HOME

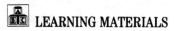 PARTY

 LEARNING MATERIALS

SCHOOL/ORGANIZATION

PROFESSIONAL

What's in This Section

Ideas! Ideas! Ideas! The handbook's design pages contain hundreds and hundreds of ideas. For your convenience, the designs are organized into five categories: *Home, Party, Learning Materials, School/Organization, Professional.* Each category is further organized by topic such as letterheads, cards, signs, or flyers. Every page is clearly marked so that you can find the design idea you're looking for easily and quickly!

The handbook's designs show a wide variety of approaches to *The Print Shop.* Together as a group, the designs stretch the limits of *The Print Shop* and broaden the range of what you can do. Highlighted for you here is an overview of what you'll find in this section.

New Ideas for Old Applications: You'll find a large assortment of signs, greeting cards, letterheads and banners with different looks and styles for different purposes.

New Applications: Using the four basic Print Shop modes, you'll find designs for more than 25 unique items such as ads, business cards and wrapping paper.

Ideas for Combining Modes: You'll find many sample designs created from a single powerful concept–use two different Print Shop modes together or the same mode twice.

Designer Techniques: You'll find easy-to-copy techniques used by professional designers that can help give your own original designs a more polished look.

Design Concepts: You'll find fundamental design concepts highlighted for you to consider applying to your own original designs.

Hints, Tips and Shortcuts: You'll find 25 hints and shortcuts you can put to work for you right away.

Using This Section

If you were to count the number of designs in this section, you would come up with 111. (Not bad.) Does that mean there also are 111 ideas? Absolutely not! Many designs combine two, three or more ideas. And there are alternative ideas in the design notes on every page.

To get the most out of Designs, Designs, Designs look beyond the printed designs shown. Think of these designs as examples. They've been included not only for you to copy (which, of course, you're welcome to do!) but also to give you a sense of what can be done—Print Shop possibilities.

Highlighted for you here (and first explained on pages 6-7) are suggestions for using this section.

SUGGESTION #1. When you find a design idea you like, by all means copy it!

SUGGESTION #2. When you find a design idea you like, but it isn't quite right for your application, adapt it! Change the design. Make it work for your specific need.

SUGGESTION #3. Add your own ideas to the handbook designs. Embellish them! Edit them!

SUGGESTION #4. When you're looking for a design idea, say a sign for a garage sale, don't restrict yourself only to designs from the most obvious section: *Home.* There may very well be a sign in the *School* or *Professional* section that can be easily adapted and better suited for the garage sale sign you want to create. Keep in mind these two words: THINK MULTIPURPOSE! Consider designs from all five sections.

SUGGESTION #5. When you see a design that uses a Print Shop program you don't have, don't rule it out! In many cases, alternative choices are offered in the design notes. And you're likely to have substitution ideas of your own.

SUGGESTION #6. When you look at a design, think about the graphic best suited for your message. Substituting a graphic is easy and may be the only change needed to make a design work just right for you.

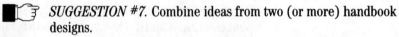 *SUGGESTION #7.* Combine ideas from two (or more) handbook designs.

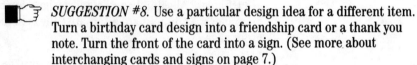 *SUGGESTION #8.* Use a particular design idea for a different item. Turn a birthday card design into a friendship card or a thank you note. Turn the front of the card into a sign. (See more about interchanging cards and signs on page 7.)

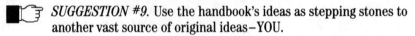 *SUGGESTION #9.* Use the handbook's ideas as stepping stones to another vast source of original ideas–YOU.

Tricks and Techniques: An Overview

Throughout this section, special techniques have been used to get greater Print Shop variety. Four techniques are worth noting with a brief explanation. Apply them to your own original work for added flexibility and more power.

■ **Combining Modes.** Many handbook designs use two different modes together (e.g., sign and letterhead) or the same mode twice. With this technique you simply work in one mode and print, then roll back your paper, work in a second mode and print again. It's a terrific way to open doors to new design possibilities. Make sure that all graphics and text fall where you want them to by marking your original print starting point with a light pencil. In this way, you can carefully control where the graphics and/or text from the second printing will appear in relationship to the first. For some designs you will want to start your second printing at the same point as your first. For other designs you may want to start higher or lower.

■ **Rolling Back Your Paper.** Rolling your paper back to its original print starting point can be done over and over again to add a variety of graphics and fonts to your design. Just remember to mark your print starting point for reference.

■ **Cutting and Pasting.** With scissors and glue at hand, *The Print Shop* possibilities are limitless. Included in the handbook are several examples of cut and pasted designs. You may not want to use the cut and pasted sample as your original–unless you're planning to send the piece to a printer for reproduction. If so, the printer will photograph your pasted up design for printing. Or, you can copy the piece on a copying machine and duplicate your pasted up design yourself.

■ **Stopping the Printer.** You're creating a sign and you want a single row of tiled figures across the top. Just make your selection for the tiled graphic pattern and turn off the printer after the first row prints. If desired, you can then roll back your paper and add your words. If you only want a portion of a graphic pattern, turn off your printer as soon as the portion you want is printed.

Getting to Know the Symbols

Every handbook design is clearly marked with easy-to-recognize symbols to let you know immediately if more than just the original Print Shop program was used to create that design. Symbols are also used if a design requires additional materials, such as scissors, or if copying on a copier is recommended. The handbook's symbols are reviewed for you here.

P The Print Shop

1 Graphics Library 1

2 Graphics Library 2

3 Graphics Library 3

H Holiday Edition

C Companion

(REMINDER: The IBM symbols appear next to the Apple and Commodore symbols only when they differ from the Apple and Commodore versions.)

✄ Scissors are required

  Copying on a copy machine is recommended

Getting to Know the Design Page

The design page comes complete with the following information:

Category (e.g., *Home*)
Topic Identification (e.g., *Letterhead*)
Print Out of the Design
What You Need

What You Do
Hints
Design Notes

Each of these elements is called out and explained on the reduced sample design page shown on page 26.

Getting to Know the Pattern Abbreviations

Step-by-step instructions that reflect the order of Print Shop choice screens are included for every design right on the design page under the heading What You Do. These instructions use easy-to-follow pattern abbreviations. As you move through the Print Shop screens the pattern abbreviations will be much more obvious. Your design choices can be made quickly and easily.

All pattern abbreviations are outlined on pages 27-29. Refer back to this section whenever you're not sure what a particular abbreviation represents in a pattern.

Counting Lines in the Handbook Designs

All line numbers in the step-by-step design instructions refer to line numbers in *the small font size only.* If a design calls for a font in the large size, you're instructed to go to a particular line of the small font size and then change the font size of that line to large. By pressing CTRL-S to enlarge the font, the line occupies *two lines* of the small font size (see illustrations on next page). To follow the handbook's design instructions, count each line on screen marked for the small font size as *one line*, and each line on screen marked for the large size as *two lines*. (Note: The program is preset for the small font size. Unless you indicate to change the font size of a particular line, the line is in the small font size and should be counted as one line.)

Changing Font Size in the Handbook Designs

Whenever a handbook design calls for a font in the large size, the pattern abbreviation **CH SIZE:L** appears in the step-by-step instructions in parentheses next to the appropriate line number. (See Pattern Abbreviations, page 27). To call up the font in the large size,

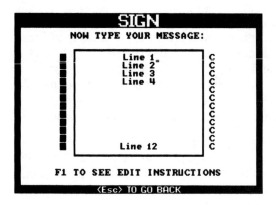

simply enter the text that belongs on that line and then press CTRL-S *right after.* Or, if you prefer, you can press CTRL-S *right before* entering your text for that line.

When two (or more) lines call for a font in the large size, a *single* abbreviation for CH SIZE:L may appear in parenthesis next to both line numbers. For example, if a design calls for Lines 1 and 3 in the large font size, the design instructions will read: **L1,L3 (CH SIZE:L) text.** To be sure your text sits in the correct position in the design, change the font size for each line either *right after or right before* you enter your text for that line. Complete each line before going on to the next. In the above example, enter your text for Line 1, press CTRL-S and then move on to Line 3. Or, press CTRL-S with the cursor on Line 1, enter your text for Line 1 and then move on to Line 3. As long as the change of font size to large for Line 1 is indicated before you begin entering your text for Line 3, your words will sit in the same position as in the handbook design.

About the Print Starting Point

Handbook designs that mix fonts and graphics take advantage of added design power that comes with using two different modes together or the same mode twice, three times or more.

Inputting designs that combine modes is easy – a full set of instructions is included. As indicated, simply mark your original print starting point in light pencil. (We recommend placing your mark near the paper holding bar of your printer approximately 1/4 inch above the folding line of your paper.) Always start with a lead-in sheet to mark. If your lead-in sheet is not blank and contains a design or information you want to use, just be certain your pencil mark is *very* light—for erasing without a trace! Also, for easier measuring, use a clear plastic ruler that is flexible and bends.

The exact position of your print starting mark is not at all critical. But try to be consistent. By always placing your mark in the same spot, you'll be able to find your original print starting point quickly and easily when instructed to roll back your paper.

Some designs require you to roll back your paper to your original print starting point. For these designs, simply roll back your paper to the exact same position as your original printing position. Other designs require that you roll back your paper to a position *below* your original print starting point. For these designs, roll back your paper to your original print starting point and then roll your paper *forward* the indicated amount. For designs that require you to roll back your paper to a position *above* your original print starting point, roll back to your original print starting point and then roll your paper *backward* the indicated amount.

About Hardware Variations

All the handbook designs can be created on an Apple, Commodore or IBM system. The designs shown in the book were created on an Apple system with an ImageWriter printer. Designs created with a Commodore system or IBM system will look slightly different. Even designs created with another Apple configuration may look different from the printed handbook samples. Don't be alarmed! There is not one right way for the designs to look. All the designs, except where noted, have been tested and adapted to work for a variety of systems —each with its own unique style.

Hints, Tips and Shortcuts

Hints, tips and shortcuts are all over the Print Shop handbook! Turn to any page and you're likely to find at least one of the three. In the design section there are hints for designing. In the art section there are hints for creating new graphics. And for giving old graphics a new look. In the planning section there are hints for organizing your design ideas.

Some of the handbook hints are very specific and have limited application. Others are much broader. The 25 hints and tips with the broadest application are highlighted here. Whenever and wherever appropriate–put them to work for you!

Hint #1: Mix fonts and graphics! Roll back your paper to combine two modes together or use the same mode two, three times or more!

Hint #2: Mark your original print starting point in light pencil when combining modes. Then when you're all done, simply erase your mark.

Hint #3: ESCAPE back to the menus you want to change after you print and want to use the same mode again. It's likely to be faster than starting from scratch.

Hint #4: Mixing fonts is easier if you select fonts with the same number of lines per page.

Hint #5: Print a column of graphics down the left side of your page with the Graphic Editor (see example on page 125).

Hint #6: Liven up your designs–use brightly colored markers to color in graphics or words in an outline font. Transparent highlight markers work well.

Hint #7: Customize the tiled pattern! Print as many rows of a graphic as you want and then simply turn off your printer.

Hint #8: Combine borders–print one border, then roll back your paper and add another.

Hint #9: Superimpose one graphic over another graphic that has large open spaces inside. A large-sized graphic, a medium-sized graphic in Custom (3) position and a small-sized graphic in Custom (7) position all sit in the same place on the page.

Hint #10: Cut and paste your graphics and words. Add type and graphics from other sources to your pasted up design for even greater variety. Then copy on a copying machine or take to a local print shop.

Hint #11: For quick ruled lines–use the "dash" key repeatedly.

Hint #12: Add descriptive information to signs, flyers and ads using the address lines of the letterhead mode.

Hint #13: For a short note–use the Typewriter font in the sign mode.

Hint #14: Stack several banners on top of one another to create an "oversized sign."

Hint #15: Several banners can also be attached at the side or "chained" to create a very long banner.

Hint #16: Create an "oversized sign" from several 8½ x 11 signs. Attach two separate signs at top and bottom to create a stronger, single statement or put several signs together horizontally for longer messages. Several sheets of a repeat pattern can be used to frame your sign.

Hint #17: Wallpaper a bulletin board or part of a wall with several sheets of the same design. Print the design several times or copy your original on a copying machine.

Hint #18: Let a copying machine mix Print Shop modes for you. Print one part of your design on one sheet of paper, print the second part on another sheet. Then copy your first design on a copier. Take the copied sheet and place it in position to run back through the copier. Now copy the second part of your design right on to this sheet. Your copier has just combined modes!

Hint #19: Leave extra space between your letters and words for greater interest and readability.

Hint #20: Use a joystick or KoalaPad, if one is available, in the Graphic Editor to fill in or erase large areas of a graphic. You're sure to save time.

Hint #21: When inputting the handbook's art, don't be concerned if you don't match every single dot. Even if 90% of your dots match up, your graphic is sure to look like the handbook's.

Hint #22: Certain Print Shop graphics (#51-#60 App/Comm–#121-#140 IBM) are included for tiled patterns. However, you may have broader use for these graphics in your designs. For greater flexibility, call one up in the Graphic Editor, save it on a personal disk and then use in a design as any other graphic–choose small, medium or large size and the layout of your choice.

Hint #23: The greeting card and sign modes offer the exact same choices for positioning text and graphics. One design idea works for both! One set of templates also works for both!

Hint #24: Save time–refer to The Fonts section when planning your message. You'll see approximately how many letters will fit on a line.

Hint #25: Sit back, "think something different" and *have fun!*

The Design Page

The design page includes a great deal more than a sample design. The reduced page shown here provides an explanation of the various elements you'll find with every handbook design.

Topic Identification: Identifies the specific item such as *letterhead* shown here.

What You Need: Easy-to-recognize symbols (shown on page 10) tell you what Print Shop programs were used to create the design.

What You Do: Step-by-step instructions lead you through the design every step of the way. A complete listing of pattern abbreviations is shown on pages 27-29.

Category Symbol: Symbol at top right tells you if you're in the *Home, School/Organization, Party, Learning Materials,* or *Professional* section.

Hints: Includes shortcuts and suggestions for working on the design.

Design Notes: A variety of information may appear here. For example, there may be alternative design suggestions, alternative graphic choices, a simplified way to create a similar looking design, or an explanation of a design concept or technique.

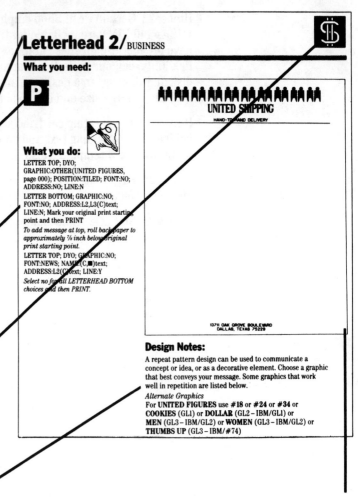

The Design: An actual reduced print out of what you'll get is shown here.

The Pattern Abbreviations

Most of the pattern abbreviations are self-explanatory when working side-by-side with *The Print Shop* program. However, if a pattern abbreviation stumps you, just refer back to this section.

Functions shared by greeting cards, signs, letterheads and banners are included in the section For All Items. Functions specific to an item are listed separately by item.

FOR ALL ITEMS

DESIGN YOUR OWN	DYO
BORDERS	BORDER:
Thin Line	THIN
Double Line	DOUBLE
Thick Line	THICK
Beads	BEAD
Lattice	LATTICE
Floral	FLORAL
Stars	STAR
Hearts	HEART
Wicker	WICKER
From Other Disk	OTHER – *For options: See "From Other Disk"*
No Border	NO
From Other Disk	OTHER:
Graphics Library 1	GL1: Name (IBM/GL— *-if different*)
Graphics Library 2	GL2: Name (IBM/GL— *-if different*)
Graphics Library 3	GL3: Name (IBM/GL— -)
Holiday Edition	HE
IBM Program Disk	IBM
Original Art	ORIG: Name, page ____
Modified Art	MOD: Name, page ____
GRAPHIC	GRAPHIC:
By Number	BY # ( )
From Other Disk	OTHER – *For options: See "From Other Disk"*
No Graphic	NO
GRAPHIC SIZE	SIZE:
Small	SM
Medium	MED
Large	LG
GRAPHIC LAYOUT	LAYOUT:
Staggered	STAGGERED
Tiled	TILED
Custom Layout	CUSTOM(#, #, #,...)
If Custom Layout:	
(for small) numbers 1-13	1-13
(for medium) numbers 1-5	1-5

FONTS	FONT:
RSVP	RSVP
ALEXIA	ALEXIA
NEWS	NEWS
TECH	TECH
PARTY	PARTY
BLOCK	BLOCK
TYPEWRITER	TYPEWRITER
STENCIL	STENCIL
From Other Disk	OTHER — *For options: See "From Other Disk"*
None	NO
MESSAGE	MESSAGE:
Line 1	L1 *(text)*
Line 2	L2 *(text)*
Line 3	L3 *(text)*
etc.	etc.
POSITION OF TEXT	
C Center	C
L Left	L
R Right	R
CHANGE FORM OF LINE	
■ Solid	■
☐ Outline	☐
3-D	3D
CHANGE SIZE OF LINE TO LARGE	CH SIZE: L

GREETING CARD	CARD
FRONT	FRONT
Border	*(see FOR ALL ITEMS)*
Graphic	*(see FOR ALL ITEMS)*
Graphic Size	*(see FOR ALL ITEMS)*
Graphic Layout	*(see FOR ALL ITEMS)*
Message	*(see FOR ALL ITEMS)*
Center TOP to BOTTOM	CENTER:
Yes	Y
No	N
INSIDE	INSIDE
(Same as FRONT)	

SIGN	SIGN
Border	*(see FOR ALL ITEMS)*
Graphic	*(see FOR ALL ITEMS)*
Graphic Size	*(see FOR ALL ITEMS)*

Graphic Layout	*(see FOR ALL ITEMS)*
Message	*(see FOR ALL ITEMS)*
Center TOP to BOTTOM	CENTER:
Yes	Y
No	N

LETTERHEAD LETTER

TOP	TOP
Graphic	*(see FOR ALL ITEMS)*
GRAPHIC POSITION:	POSITION:
Left Corner	LEFT
Right Corner	RIGHT
Both Corners	BOTH
Row of Six	SIX
Tiled	TILED
FONT	*(see FOR ALL ITEMS)*
NAME Line	NAME: *(type name)*
ADDRESS Line	ADDRESS:
Line 1	L1 *(text)*
Line 2	L2 *(text)*
Line 3	L3 *(text)*
POSITION OF TEXT	
Left	L
Center	C
Right	R
DRAW LINE SEPARATING	LINE:
Yes	Y
No	N
BOTTOM	BOTTOM
(same as TOP)	

BANNER BANNER

FONT	*(see FOR ALL ITEMS)*
MESSAGE	
FORM OF FONT	
Solid	S
Outline	O
GRAPHIC	*(see FOR ALL ITEMS)*
GRAPHIC POSITION	POSITION:
Before Message	BEFORE
After Message	AFTER
Both	BOTH

Calendar/MONTHLY

What you need:

What you do:

CALENDAR; MONTHLY;
GRAPHIC:OTHER(GL2:CAMP);
POSITION:BOTH; YEAR:text;
MONTH:text;
FONT:COMPANION(BALLOON);
MESSAGE:L1(■),L2(□); CENTER:text;
BOTTOM:text; PRINT

Hints:

Note the use of large and small type within the calendar. The large type communicates emphasis and helps create a well designed calendar that is easier to read.

JULY

1988

SUN	MON	TUE	WED	THU	FRI	SAT
					1	2
3	4 HOLIDAY PICNIC	5	6	7 PACK KIDS' STUFF STOP OFF AT K-MART FOR LAST-MINUTE STUFF	8	9 KIDS TO CAMP
10 REST!	11 BRIDGE CLUB MARGIE'S BRING PRIZES	12	13 ANNIVERSARY! DINNER AT JEAN-PAUL'S	14	15	16
17 KIDS BACK FROM CAMP PICK UP AT CHURCH 2 P.M.	18	19	20	21 LAURA'S PIANO LESSON 11:00	22	23 SWIMMING PARTY AT WILSONS BRING DRINKS AND CHIPS 4 P.M.
24	25 GEORGE OFF!	26	27 DEADLINE FOR CAR INSURANCE RENEWAL (UGH!)	28	29 TINA'S BIRTHDAY! 4!	30
31						

✳✳SUMMERTIME FUN AT THE STEWARTS!!✳✳

Design Notes:

The Print Shop Companion offers many new tools. One of the most useful features is the calendar. It is simple to use and makes it so easy for you to create a "typeset" personalized calendar. Also note the weekly calendar shown in Professional applications, page 111.

Card 1/ANNIVERSARY

What you need:

P **1** **2**

(App/ Comm only)

What you do:

CARD FRONT; DYO; BORDER:STAR;
GRAPHIC:OTHER(GL1:SNOW); SIZE:SM;
LAYOUT:TILED; FONT:PARTY;
MESSAGE:L1(C,■)text,L3(C,■,CH
SIZE:L)text,L6,L8(C,■)text; CENTER:Y

CARD INSIDE; BORDER:HEART;
GRAPHIC:OTHER(GL1:FLOWERS);
SIZE:MED; LAYOUT:CUSTOM(5);
FONT:NEWS; MESSAGE:L1-L5(L,■)text;
CENTER:N; Mark your original print
starting point and then PRINT

*To add WEDDING graphic, roll back
paper to original print starting point.*
CARD FRONT; DYO; BORDER:NO;
GRAPHIC:OTHER(GL2:WEDDING–
IBM/GL1); SIZE:SM;
LAYOUT:CUSTOM(1,3,11,13); FONT:NO

*Select NO for all CARD INSIDE choices
and then PRINT.*

Card Front

Card Inside

MAY THE NEXT
50 YEARS BE
JUST AS
LOVING AND
HAPPY!

Design Notes:

For a simpler and cleaner look leave off either wedding figures
or background pattern.

Alternate Text
Card Front: HAPPY ANNIVERSARY!
Card Inside: MAY YOU HAVE MANY MORE TO COME!

Alternate Graphics
For **SNOW** use **FLOWERS** (#59 – IBM/#129)
For **FLOWERS** use **WEDDING** (GL2 – IBM/GL1) or **#16**
For **WEDDING** use **#11** or **BOUQUET** (GL3 – IBM/GL2)

Card 2/ BABY ANNOUNCEMENT

What you need:

What you do:

CARD FRONT; DYO; BORDER:FLORAL;
GRAPHIC:BY#(5); SIZE:SM;
LAYOUT:TILED; FONT:NEWS;
MESSAGE:L1(C,■,CH SIZE:L)text;
L4,L6,L8(C,■) text; CENTER:Y

CARD INSIDE; BORDER:FLORAL;
GRAPHIC:OTHER(GL2:BABY – IBM/GL1);
SIZE:SM; LAYOUT:CUSTOM(1,3,11,13);
FONT:NEWS; MESSAGE: L1-L8(C,■)text;
CENTER:Y; PRINT

Hints:

To plan your Card Inside message, refer
to The Fonts on page 255.

Card Front

Card Inside

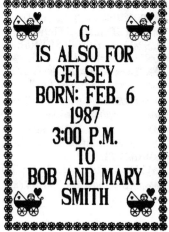

Design Notes:

The stork and baby graphic are generic and can be used for
both female and male. For names that do not begin with a "G"
for girl or "B" for boy, simply delete the word "also" from the
Card Inside message.

Alternate Text
Card Front: THE TIME HAS COME!
Card Inside: TO ANNOUNCE THE BIRTH
OF_____

Alternate Graphics
For #5 use **CHICK** (GLI) or #37 or #19
For **BABY** use #43

Card 3/BIRTHDAY

What you need:

Card Front

Card Inside

What you do:

CARD FRONT; DYO; BORDER:DOUBLE;
GRAPHIC:BY#(59–IBM/129); SIZE:SM;
LAYOUT:TILED; FONT:PARTY;
MESSAGE:L1,L3(C,■,CH SIZE:L)text;
CENTER:N

CARD INSIDE; BORDER:NO;
GRAPHIC:BY#(19); SIZE:SM;
LAYOUT:TILED; FONT:NEWS;
MESSAGE:L1-L8(C,■)text; CENTER:Y;
Mark your original print starting point
and then PRINT

*To add GIFT BOX graphic, roll back
paper to original print starting point.*

CARD FRONT; DYO; BORDER:NO:
GRAPHIC:OTHER(MOD:GIFT BOX, page
185), SIZE:LG; FONT:NO

*Select NO for all CARD INSIDE choices
and then PRINT.*

Design Notes:

Many patterns will work for this Card Front. The modified
GIFT BOX works well because it is simple enough to show off
the background. You may want to color the GIFT BOX with
markers or crayons.

Alternate Graphics
For **GIFT BOX** use #4
For **#59**(IBM/129) use **#56**(IBM/126) or **SNOW** (GL1)
For **#19** use **FLOWERS** (GL1) or **RAINBOW** (GL1)

Card 4/ BIRTHDAY/ CHILD

What you need:

What you do:

CARD FRONT; DYO; BORDER:HEART;
GRAPHIC:BY#(59 – IBM/129); SIZE:SM;
LAYOUT:TILED; FONT:BLOCK;
MESSAGE(1 space between all
letters):L1-L3,L5-L7,L9-L11(C,■)text;
CENTER:Y

CARD INSIDE; BORDER:NO;
GRAPHIC:BY#(42); SIZE:MED;
LAYOUT:CUSTOM(3,4); FONT:BLOCK;
MESSAGE:L1,L2(C,■)text; CENTER:N;
Mark your original print starting point
and then PRINT

*To add sun graphic, roll back paper to
original print starting point.*

CARD FRONT; DYO; BORDER:NO;
GRAPHIC:NO; FONT:NO

CARD INSIDE; BORDER:NO;
GRAPHIC:BY#(19); SIZE:MED;
LAYOUT:CUSTOM(5); FONT:NO; PRINT

Card Front

Card Inside

Design Notes:

For a simpler design that does not require rolling back paper,
use the same graphic in all three positions of the Card Inside.
Many Print Shop graphics are well suited for coloring.

Alternate Text
Card Inside: BRING US TO LIFE WITH COLOR!

Alternate Graphics
For #42 use #47 or **SOCCER** (GL2 – IBM/GL1)
For #19 use #41 or **PLANE** (GL2)

Card 5/CHRISTMAS

What you need:

What you do:

CARD FRONT; DYO; BORDER:THIN;
GRAPHIC:NO; FONT:ALEXIA;
MESSAGE:L1,L3(C,■,CH SIZE:L)text;
CENTER:N

CARD INSIDE;
BORDER:OTHER(HE:RIBBON2);
GRAPHIC:OTHER(HE:TOYS); SIZE:LG;
FONT:PARTY; MESSAGE:L1,L2(R,■)text,
L10(IBM/9)(C,■)text; CENTER:N; Mark
your original print starting point and
then PRINT

*To add LIGHTS (IBM/CANDLE2)
graphic, roll back paper to
approximately 2⅞ inches below original
print starting point.*

CARD FRONT; DYO; BORDER:NO;
GRAPHIC:OTHER(HE:LIGHTS –
IBM/CANDLE2); SIZE:SM;
LAYOUT:TILED; FONT:NO

*Select NO for all CARD INSIDE choices
and then PRINT. (Note: Turn off printer
after third row of graphic prints and
then press ESC (←/Comm.) to exit print
mode.*

Card Front

Card Inside

Design Notes:

The design trick of printing a tiled pattern of graphics on only
part of a card creates a very different effect and allows for
greater readability of a message.

Alternate Graphics
For **TOYS** use **#36** or **TREE** (GL1)
For **LIGHTS** (IBM/CANDLE2) use **#13** or **TREE TILE**
(GL3 – IBM/GL2)

Card 6/FRIENDSHIP

What you need:

What you do:

CARD FRONT; DYO; BORDER:DOUBLE;
GRAPHIC:OTHER(GL1:ELEPHANT);
SIZE:SM; LAYOUT:TILED;
FONT:STENCIL; MESSAGE:L4,L6,L8
(C,■,CH SIZE:L)text; CENTER:Y

CARD INSIDE; BORDER:LATTICE;
GRAPHIC:NO; FONT:NEWS;
MESSAGE:L2,L6,L7(C,■)text;
CENTER:N; Mark your original print
starting point and then PRINT

*To add additional text to CARD INSIDE,
roll back paper to original print
starting point.*

CARD FRONT; DYO; BORDER:NO;
GRAPHIC:NO; FONT:NO; CENTER:N

CARD INSIDE; BORDER:THIN;
GRAPHIC:NO; FONT:ALEXIA;
MESSAGE:L3(C,■,CH SIZE:L)text,
L8(C,■)text; CENTER:N; PRINT

Card Front

Card Inside

Design Notes:

Combining fonts in cards adds interest to a design. Different
borders can be used to convey different messages. For example,
this combined border implies a more formal relationship
than a border such as HEARTS.

Alternate Graphics
For **ELEPHANT** use **#18** or **#25** or **REMEMBER**
(GL3 – IBM/GL2)

Card 7/FRIENDSHIP

What you need:

What you do:

CARD FRONT; DYO; BORDER:THIN;
GRAPHIC:BY#(2); SIZE:SM;
LAYOUT:TILED; FONT:BLOCK;
MESSAGE(1 space between all
letters):L1,L5(C,□,CH SIZE:L)text;
CENTER:Y

CARD INSIDE; BORDER:HEART;
GRAPHIC:OTHER(ORIG:HANDS, page
166); SIZE:SM; LAYOUT:TILED;
FONT:BLOCK; MESSAGE(1 space
between all letters):L1,L5(C,□,CH
SIZE:L)text; CENTER:Y; PRINT

Card Front

Card Inside

Design Notes:

For Card Inside message use Block font in solid instead
of outline.

Alternate Graphics
For #2 use **HEART** (mod. ART, page 186)
For **HANDS** use #53 (IBM/#123)

Card 8/GET WELL

What you need:

What you do:

CARD FRONT; DYO; BORDER:WICKER;
GRAPHIC:BY#(52 – IBM/122); SIZE:SM;
LAYOUT:TILED; FONT:BLOCK;
MESSAGE:L1,L13(IBM/L11)(C,■,CH
SIZE:L)text; CENTER:Y

CARD INSIDE; BORDER:DOUBLE;
GRAPHIC:BY#(59 – IBM/129); SIZE:SM;
LAYOUT:TILED; FONT:BLOCK;
MESSAGE:L1,L3,L5,L7(C,■,CH SIZE:L)
text, L12,L13(IBM/L11,L12)(C,■)text;
CENTER:Y; Mark your original print
starting point and then PRINT

*To add VAMPIRE graphic, roll back
paper to original print starting point.*

CARD FRONT; DYO; BORDER:NO;
GRAPHIC:OTHER(GL3:VAMPIRE–
IBM/GL2); SIZE:LG; FONT:NO

*Select NO for all CARD INSIDE choices
and then PRINT.*

Card Front

Card Inside

Design Notes:

The background pattern on Card Front can be deleted
for a cleaner look.

Alternate Text
Card Front: I MISS YOU!
Card Inside: GET WELL SOON!

Alternate Graphics
For **VAMPIRE** use **MIME** (GL1) or **DOG** (GL1)
For **#59**(IBM/129) use **#2** or **SNOW** (GL1)

Card 9/GRADUATION

What you need:

Card Inside

Card Front

What you do:

CARD FRONT; DYO; BORDER:STAR;
GRAPHIC:BY#(6); SIZE:MED;
LAYOUT:CUSTOM(3); FONT:NEWS;
MESSAGE:L1-L4(C,■)text; CENTER:N

CARD INSIDE; BORDER:BEAD;
GRAPHIC:OTHER(GL1:PARTY); SIZE:SM;
LAYOUT:CUSTOM(1,3,12); FONT:STENCIL;
MESSAGE:L4(C,■,CH SIZE:L)text;
CENTER:N; Mark your original print
starting point and then PRINT

*To add text to CARD FRONT and
graphics to CARD INSIDE, roll back
paper to original print starting point.*

CARD FRONT; DYO; BORDER:NO;
GRAPHIC:NO; FONT:STENCIL;
MESSAGE:L11,L13(C,□,CH SIZE:L)text;
CENTER:N

CARD INSIDE; BORDER:NO;
GRAPHIC:OTHER(GL1:PARTY2);
SIZE:SM; LAYOUT:CUSTOM(2,11,13);
FONT:BLOCK; MESSAGE:L6(C,■,CH
SIZE:L)text; CENTER:N; PRINT

*To add text to CARD INSIDE, roll back
paper to original print starting point.*

CARD FRONT; DYO; BORDER:NO;
GRAPHIC:NO; FONT:NO

CARD INSIDE; BORDER:NO;
GRAPHIC:NO; FONT:PARTY;
MESSAGE:L8(IBM/L7)(C,■)text;
CENTER:N; PRINT

Design Notes:

Mixing graphics and fonts through multiple printings creates
interesting effects. You may want to simplify this Card Inside
by using one font and one graphic. Print your card on colored
paper or fill in graduate circle background with a brightly
colored marker.

Alternate Graphics
For #6 use #38 or CERTIFICATE (GL3 – IBM/#88)
For PARTY use BEACH (GL2)
For PARTY2 use #16

Card 10/ HALLOWEEN

What you need:

Card Front

Card Inside

What you do:

CARD FRONT; DYO; BORDER:THIN;
GRAPHIC:BY#(52 – IBM/122); SIZE:SM;
LAYOUT:TILED; FONT:BLOCK;
MESSAGE:L1-L2,L12-L14(IBM/L10-
L12)(C,■)text; CENTER:Y

CARD INSIDE; BORDER:WICKER;
GRAPHIC:BY#(7); SIZE:SM;
LAYOUT:TILED; FONT:RSVP;
MESSAGE:L1(C,■)text; CENTER:Y; Mark
your original print starting point and
then PRINT

*To add pumpkin graphic, roll back
paper to original print starting point.*

CARD FRONT; DYO; BORDER:NO;
GRAPHIC:BY#(7); SIZE:LG; FONT:NO

*Select NO for all CARD INSIDE choices
and then PRINT.*

Design Notes:

Substitute graphics and use this same card design for
other holidays.

Alternate Graphics
For **CHRISTMAS** use #10 and SNOW (GL1)
For **CHANUKAH** use #8 and SNOW (GL1)
For **VALENTINE'S DAY** use #2 and #52(IBM/122)

Card 11/MOTHER'S DAY

What you need:

Card Front

Card Inside

> THANK YOU
> FOR ALWAYS
> BEING THERE,
> MAKING LIFE
> A LITTLE
> EASIER,
> AND
> FOR JUST BEING
> YOU!

What you do:

CARD FRONT; DYO; BORDER:DOUBLE;
GRAPHIC:BY#(56–IBM/126); SIZE:SM;
LAYOUT:TILED; FONT:RSVP; MESSAGE:
L1–L3(L,■)text; CENTER:N

CARD INSIDE; BORDER:DOUBLE;
GRAPHIC:BY#(2); SIZE:SM;
LAYOUT:CUSTOM(1,3,11,13);
FONT:BLOCK; MESSAGE:L1-L9(C,■)text;
CENTER:Y; Mark your original print
starting point and then PRINT

To add BIRD graphic, roll back paper to
approximately 1 inch below original
print starting point.

CARD FRONT; DYO; BORDER:NO;
GRAPHIC:OTHER(ORIG:BIRD,
page 156); SIZE:LG; FONT:NO

Select NO for all CARD INSIDE choices
and then PRINT.

Design Notes:

This card design works equally well for Father's Day.

Alternate Text
Card Front: #1 MOM!
Card Inside: HAPPY MOTHER'S DAY TO THE BEST MOM
OF ALL!

Alternate Graphics
For **#56**(IBM/126) use **#59**(IBM/129)
For **#2** use **BIRD** (Orig. Art, page 156)

Card 12/VALENTINE

What you need:

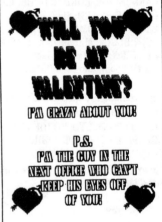

What you do:

CARD FRONT; DYO; BORDER:HEART;
GRAPHIC:OTHER(GL1:RAINBOW);
SIZE:SM; LAYOUT:TILED; FONT:ALEXIA;
MESSAGE:L1-L3,L6-L8(C,■)text;
CENTER:Y

CARD INSIDE; BORDER:THIN;
GRAPHIC:OTHER(MOD:HEART,
page 186); SIZE:SM;
LAYOUT:CUSTOM(1,3,11,13);
FONT:STENCIL;
MESSAGE:L1,L3,L5(C,3D,CH SIZE:L)text,
L7,L10-L14(C,□)text; CENTER:Y; Mark
your original print starting point and
then PRINT

*To add cupid graphic, roll back paper to
original print starting point.*

CARD FRONT; DYO; BORDER:NO;
GRAPHIC:BY#(12); SIZE:MED;
LAYOUT:CUSTOM(3); FONT:NO

*Select NO for all CARD INSIDE choices
and then PRINT.*

Design Notes:

For a simpler design eliminate the background pattern on the
Card Front and use only the single centered graphic. Or include
the background pattern and eliminate the centered graphic.

Alternate Graphics
For **HEART** *use* #2 or #4 or #12 or **GIFT BOX** (Mod. Art,
page 185)
For **RAINBOW** use #11 or #12 without centered graphic

Diary 1/ADULT

What you need:

What you do:

SIGN; DYO; BORDER:NO;
GRAPHIC:OTHER(ORIG:NOTE LINES,
page 169); SIZE:SM; LAYOUT:TILED;
FONT:NO; Mark your usual print
starting point, roll your paper forward
approximately 4⅜ inches from this point
and PRINT (Note: Turn off printer when
line at bottom of page prints)

*To add JOURNAL, roll back paper to
usual print starting point.*

SIGN; DYO; BORDER:NO; GRAPHIC:NO;
FONT:NEWS; MESSAGE(1 space between
all letters):L3(C,■)text; CENTER:N;
PRINT

*To add INITIALS crest graphic, roll back
paper to approximately ½ inch below
usual print starting point.*

SIGN; DYO; BORDER:NO;
GRAPHIC:OTHER(MOD:INITIALS, page
195); SIZE:SM; LAYOUT:CUSTOM(1);
FONT:NO; PRINT

*To add date information, roll back
paper to approximately ¼ inch above
usual print starting point.*

LETTER TOP; DYO; GRAPHIC:NO;
FONT:NO; ADDRESS:L1(1 space between
all letters)(R)text, L3(R)text; LINE:N

*Select NO for all LETTERHEAD BOTTOM
choices and then PRINT.*

*To add your initials, print on a separate
sheet of paper and then paste up.*

LETTER TOP; DYO; GRAPHIC:NO;
FONT:NO; ADDRESS:L1 (1 space between
all letters)(C)text; LINE:N

*Select NO for all LETTERHEAD BOTTOM
choices and then PRINT. Be sure to print
on a separate sheet of paper. Then cut
and paste initials into the initial crest of
your diary page design and copy on a
copying machine or print at a quick
print shop.*

TODAY'S DATE:

JOURNAL

Design Notes:

This design in multiples is well suited for a notebook of
memoirs. The additional effort to include your initials adds
a strong personal touch. However, for faster results replace
the INITIALS crest with a different graphic.

Alternate Graphics

For **INITIALS** crest use **#35** or **#40** or **ART** (GL1) or
WRITER (GL1) or **THINKER** (GL1) or **TIME** (GL2)

Diary 2/CHILD

What you need:

What you do: ✍

SIGN; DYO; BORDER:THIN;
GRAPHIC:OTHER(MOD:ROCKER,
page 200), SIZE:SM;
LAYOUT:CUSTOM(11,12,13);
FONT:TYPEWRITER; MESSAGE:L1(C,■)
text, L5,L6(L,■)text, L7,L9,L11,L13(C,■)
text, L8,L10,L12(L,■)text; CENTER:Y;
Mark your original print starting point
and then PRINT

*To add BEAR graphic, roll back your
paper to approximately ¾ inch below
original print starting point.*

SIGN; DYO; BORDER:NO;
GRAPHIC:OTHER(ORIG:BEAR, page 155);
SIZE:SM; LAYOUT:CUSTOM(2);
FONT:NO; PRINT

```
        DELSEY'S  DAILY  DIARY

   YEAR:
   DAY:

   ------------------------

   ------------------------

   ------------------------

   ------------------------

   ------------------------

   ------------------------

   ------------------------
```

Design Notes:

This design is easy to create and shows how the "dash"
key of the keyboard can be used to create notepaper lines.
Substituting graphics can quickly alter the look of the design
and the age appropriateness.

Alternate Graphics
For **BEAR** use #27 or #43
For **ROCKER** use **MR SUN** (GL3 – IBM/GL2) or
KEYBOARD (GL2)

Flyer 1/SALE

What you need:

*(App/
Comm only)*

What you do:

*Note: Instructions are for Apple/
Commodore only. Adapt selection and
placement of fonts for IBM.*

SIGN; DYO; BORDER:WICKER;
GRAPHIC:OTHER(GL3:RIGHT); SIZE:SM;
LAYOUT:CUSTOM(1); FONT:BLOCK;
MESSAGE:L1,L6(C,■)text; L4(C,□,CH
SIZE:L)text, L8,L10,L12(L,■)text;
CENTER:N; Mark your original print
starting point and then PRINT

*To add LEFT pointing graphic and
additional text, roll back paper to
original print starting point.*

SIGN; DYO; BORDER:NO;
GRAPHIC:OTHER(GL3:LEFT); SIZE:SM;
LAYOUT:CUSTOM(3);
FONT:TYPEWRITER;
MESSAGE:L3(C,■)text,
L8,L10,L12(indent appropriate number of
spaces)(C,■)text; CENTER:N; PRINT

*To add second line of text, roll back
paper to original print starting point.*

SIGN; DYO; BORDER:NO; GRAPHIC:NO;
FONT:STENCIL; MESSAGE:L2(C,■)text;
CENTER:N; PRINT

*To add text at bottom, roll back paper to
approximately ¾ inch above original
print starting point.*

LETTER TOP; DYO; GRAPHIC:NO;
FONT:NO; ADDRESS:NO; LINE:N

LETTER BOTTOM; GRAPHIC:NO;
FONT:ALEXIA; NAME:(C,■)text;
ADDRESS:L1,L2(C)text; LINE:N; PRINT

Hints:

Fill in an outline font with markers for an
extra bold headline before duplicating a
flyer.

Design Notes:

Combining fonts adds great variety to a design as well as
creating an easy-to-read format. Planning is simplified when
you select fonts with the same number of lines per page (see
About the Font Categories, page 228). Try using the HOUSE
graphic (MOD. ART, page 187) or #31 for a different look.
With this substitution the graphics at left and right can both
be printed at the same time.

Flyer 2/EVENT

What you need:

What you do:

SIGN; DYO; BORDER:STAR;
GRAPHIC:OTHER(GL1:CLOWN);
SIZE:MED; LAYOUT:CUSTOM(3);
FONT:PARTY; MESSAGE(1 space
between all letters):L3(C,■)text;
CENTER:N; Mark your original print
starting point and then PRINT

*To add PARTY graphic, roll back paper
to approximately ¾ inch above original
print starting point.*

SIGN; DYO; BORDER:NO;
GRAPHIC:OTHER(GL1:PARTY); SIZE:SM;
LAYOUT:CUSTOM(11,12,13); FONT:NO;
PRINT

*To add text at top, roll back paper to
approximately 1 inch below original
print starting point.*

LETTER TOP; DYO; GRAPHIC:NO;
FONT:NO; ADDRESS:L1(C)text,
L3(1 space between all letters)(C)text;
LINE:N

*Select NO for all LETTERHEAD BOTTOM
choices and then PRINT.*

*To add text at bottom, roll back paper to
approximately ¾ inch above original
print starting point.*

LETTER TOP; DYO; GRAPHIC:NO;
FONT:NO; ADDRESS:NO; LINE:N

LETTER BOTTOM; GRAPHIC:NO;
FONT:NO; ADDRESS:L1(C)text;
L3(1 space between all letters, 2 spaces
between words)(C)text; LINE:N; PRINT

Design Notes:

Combining the sign and letterhead modes allows you to include small, informative text on a poster-type sign. Choose alternate graphics that reflect your event. For example, use #15 for a neighborhood event or #18 for an event that involves sharing ideas.

Flyer 3/ GARAGE SALE

What you need:

P **1** **2**
(App/ Comm only)

3 *(App/ Comm only)*

What you do:

SIGN; DYO; BORDER:NO;
GRAPHIC:OTHER(GL3:YARDSALE–
IBM/#96); SIZE:LG; FONT:NEWS;
MESSAGE:L1,L3(COMM/IBM:See note
below)(C,■,CH SIZE:L)text,
L8(COMM/IBM:L7)(C,■)text; CENTER:N;
Mark your original print starting point
and then PRINT

*To add house graphic, roll back paper to
original print starting point.*

SIGN; DYO; BORDER:NO;
GRAPHIC:BY#(31); SIZE:SM;
LAYOUT:CUSTOM(6,8); FONT:NO; PRINT

*To add CAMERA graphic, roll back paper
to original print starting point.*

SIGN; DYO; BORDER:NO;
GRAPHIC:OTHER(GL2:CAMERA–
IBM/GL1); SIZE:SM;
LAYOUT:CUSTOM(13); FONT:NO; PRINT

*To add TOOLS graphic, roll back paper
to original print starting point.*

SIGN; DYO; BORDER:NO;
GRAPHIC:OTHER(GL2:TOOLS–
IBM/GL1); SIZE:SM;
LAYOUT:CUSTOM(11); FONT:NO; PRINT

*To add message and address, roll back
paper to original print starting point.*

LETTER TOP; DYO; GRAPHIC:NO;
FONT:NO; ADDRESS:NO; LINE:NO

LETTER BOTTOM; GRAPHIC:NO;
FONT:NEWS; NAME:(C,■)text;
ADDRESS:L2,L3(C)text; LINE:N; PRINT

*Note: COMM/IBM users should print L1
and L3 separately from L8 and Yardsale
graphic. For COMM roll back paper to
approximately ¾ inch above usual print
starting point; for IBM ½ inch.*

Design Notes:

To simplify this design, eliminate the large Yardsale graphic
and print the houses with the text. The extra printings for
graphics at the bottom can be reduced by using the same
graphic in both positions at bottom.

Letterhead 1/ADULT FORMAL

What you need:

ALLEN H. BAUER

4842 NORTH ELM STREET
IRVINE, CA 92715
(000) 000-0000

What you do:

LETTER TOP; DYO; GRAPHIC:NO;
FONT:BLOCK; NAME(1 space between all
letters)(C,□):text; ADDRESS:NO; LINE:N
LETTER BOTTOM; GRAPHIC:BY#(25);
POSITION:LEFT; FONT:NO; ADDRESS:L1-
L3(R)text; LINE:Y; PRINT

Design Notes:

Try several different fonts in outline for this formal, more
sophisticated look. Also, many different graphics will work.
Choose one that best suits your personality or purpose.

Alternate Graphics
For **#25** use **#40** or **#11** or **#48** or **ART** (GL1) or **ARIES**
through **PISCES** (GL1) or **MEMO** (GL1) or an occupation such
as **ELECTRICIAN** (GL2 – IBM/GL1) or **SHELL** (GL2)

Letterhead 2/ADULT FORMAL

What you need:

What you do:

LETTER TOP; DYO; GRAPHIC:NO;
FONT:NEWS; NAME:(C,■)text; LINE:Y

LETTER BOTTOM; GRAPHIC:NO;
FONT:NO; ADDRESS: L1-L3(C)text;
LINE:N; PRINT

THOMAS G. COLLINGSWORTH

12500 KINGS POINT ROAD
PHILADELPHIA, PA 19047
(000) 000-0000

Design Notes:

This easy-to-create letterhead works well for all purposes.
You may want to add graphics to BOTH CORNERS at the top.
For graphic suggestions, see Letterhead 1, page 48.

Letterhead 3/ADULT PERSONAL

What you need:

What you do:

LETTER TOP; DYO;
GRAPHIC:OTHER(ORIG:BIRD, page
156); POSITION:RIGHT; FONT:ALEXIA;
NAME:(L,■)text; ADDRESS:NO; LINE:Y
LETTER BOTTOM; GRAPHIC:NO;
FONT:NO; ADDRESS:L1,L2(L)text;
LINE:N; PRINT

JAYNE

49 JACKSON ST.
DERBY, CT. 09880

Design Notes:

This clean and simple design works well for personal
stationery for adults or children.

Alternate Graphics
Adult: #11 or #18 or #25 or #49 or **WRITER** (GL1)
Child: #36 or #46 or **ROCKER** (GL1 or MOD. ART, page 200)
or **DANCER** (GL1)

Letterhead 4/HOME BUSINESS

What you need:

QUILTS BY AMY

3470 APPLETREE LANE, MONTPELIER, VT 02822, (000) 000-0000

What you do:

LETTER TOP; DYO; GRAPHIC:NO; FONT:RSVP; NAME(1 space between all letters, 2 spaces between words):(C,■)text; ADDRESS:NO; LINE:Y

LETTER BOTTOM; GRAPHIC:OTHER(GL1:SNOW); POSITION:TILED; FONT:NO; ADDRESS:L2(C)text; LINE:N; Mark your original print starting point and then PRINT

To add BOUQUET graphic, roll back paper to original print starting point.

LETTER TOP; DYO; GRAPHIC:NO; FONT:NO; ADDRESS:NO; LINE:N

LETTER BOTTOM; GRAPHIC:OTHER(GL3:BOUQUET – IBM/GL2); POSITION:SIX; FONT:NO; ADDRESS:NO; LINE:N; PRINT

Design Notes:

Alter the look of this design by substituting the SNOW graphic with a pattern reflecting your image. Select a pattern that will not overpower your graphic. Replace the BOUQUET with a graphic that best communicates your message.

Alternate Graphics
For **BOUQUET** use **#49** or **#11** or **BUTTERFLY** (MOD. ART, page 177)
For **SNOW** use **#53** (IBM/123)

Letterhead 5/CHILD

What you need:

What you do:

LETTER TOP; DYO; GRAPHIC:NO;
FONT: STENCIL; NAME:(C,■)text;
ADDRESS (2 spaces between
words):L1(C)text; LINE:Y

LETTER BOTTOM;
GRAPHIC:OTHER(ORIG:BEAR,
page 155); POSITION:SIX; FONT:NO;
ADDRESS:NO; LINE:N; PRINT

Design Notes:

For a simple child's letterhead choose a font appropriate to
the child's age. Block is easy to read and a good choice for a
child under the age of four. Many graphics from *The Print
Shop* program disk can be substituted for the BEAR graphic.

Alternate Graphics
For **BEAR** use **#36** or **#42** or **#43** or **#44** or **#46**

Letterhead 6/CHILD

What you need:

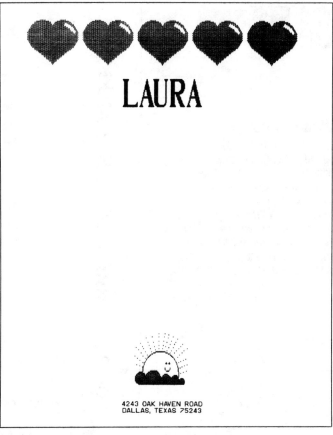

What you do:

SIGN; DYO; BORDER:NO;
GRAPHIC:BY#(2); SIZE:SM;
LAYOUT:TILED; FONT:NO; Mark your
original print starting point and then
PRINT (Note: Turn off printer as soon as
top row prints and then press ESC
(←/Comm.) to exit print mode.)

*To add sun graphic and child's name,
roll back paper to original print
starting point.*

SIGN; DYO; BORDER:NO;
GRAPHIC:BY#(19);
LAYOUT:CUSTOM(12); FONT:NEWS;
MESSAGE: L2(C,■)text; CENTER:N;
PRINT

*To add address, roll back paper to
original print starting point.*

LETTER TOP; DYO; GRAPHIC:NO;
FONT:NO; ADDRESS:NO; LINE:N

LETTER BOTTOM; GRAPHIC:NO;
FONT:NO; ADDRESS:L2,L3(C)text;
LINE:N; PRINT

Design Notes:

Many Print Shop graphics are well suited for children's
stationery. Below are suggestions.

Alternate Graphics
For #2 use #42 or **WINNER** (GL1) or **DANCER** (GL1)
For #19 use #36 or **MOON** (GL1)

Letterhead 7/CHILD

What you need:

What you do:

SIGN; DYO; BORDER:HEART;
GRAPHIC:NO; FONT:BLOCK;
MESSAGE:L4(C,□,CH SIZE:L)text;
CENTER:Y; Mark your original print
starting point and then PRINT

*To add JACK-IN-THE-BOX graphic, roll
back paper to approximately 2½ inches
above original print starting point.*

SIGN; DYO; BORDER:NO;
GRAPHIC:OTHER(ORIG:JACK-IN-THE-
BOX, page 167); SIZE:MED;
LAYOUT:CUSTOM(3); FONT:NO; PRINT

Design Notes:

Kids love to write short notes. A big, fun graphic is perfect for
a child's stationery. Copy on a copying machine for a supply
of sheets. Any graphic that is open and simple is good for
coloring and will work well.

Alternate Graphics
For **JACK-IN-THE-BOX** use **#19** or **DUCK** (GL1) or
MOON (GL1)

List 1/ GROCERY

What you need:

What you do:

SIGN; DYO; BORDER:THIN;
GRAPHIC:BY#(50); SIZE:SM;
LAYOUT:CUSTOM(2); FONT:ALEXIA;
MESSAGE:L2,L3(L-indent 1 space,■)text;
CENTER:N; Mark your original print
starting point and then PRINT

*To add NOTE LINES, roll back paper
to approximately 5 inches below your
original print starting point.*

SIGN; DYO; BORDER:NO;
GRAPHIC:OTHER(ORIG:NOTE LINES,
page 169); SIZE:SM; LAYOUT:TILED;
FONT:NO; PRINT (Note: Turn off printer
as soon as the last line within the border
prints and then press ESC (←/Comm.) to
exit print mode.)

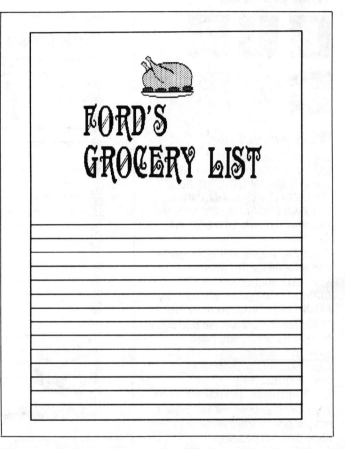

Design Notes:

The NOTE LINES pattern is simple to create and can be used
for many kinds of designs. You may want more lines for your
list. Just roll back the paper closer to the original print
starting point and choose a smaller font for your heading.

Alternate Graphics
For **#50** use **PLATE** (GL1) or **COOKING** (GL2) or **POT** (GL2)

List 2/ DAILY TO DO

What you need:

  (App/ Comm only)

What you do: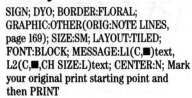

SIGN; DYO; BORDER:FLORAL;
GRAPHIC:OTHER(ORIG:NOTE LINES,
page 169); SIZE:SM; LAYOUT:TILED;
FONT:BLOCK; MESSAGE:L1(C,■)text,
L2(C,■,CH SIZE:L)text; CENTER:N; Mark
your original print starting point and
then PRINT

To add POT graphic, roll back paper to original print starting point.

SIGN; DYO; BORDER:NO;
GRAPHIC:OTHER(GL2:POT); SIZE:SM;
LAYOUT:CUSTOM(11); FONT:NO; PRINT

To add MR SUN graphic, roll back paper to original print starting point.

SIGN; DYO; BORDER:NO;
GRAPHIC:OTHER(GL3:MR SUN–
IBM/GL2); SIZE:SM;
LAYOUT:CUSTOM(12); FONT:NO; PRINT

To add MAIL graphic, roll back paper to original print starting point.

SIGN; DYO; BORDER:NO;
GRAPHIC:OTHER(GL1:MAIL); SIZE:SM;
LAYOUT:CUSTOM(13); FONT:NO; PRINT

Hints:

If you do not want lines to run through
graphics at bottom, simply turn off
printer at desired point when printing
NOTE LINES and then press ESC
(←/Comm.) to exit print mode.

Design Notes:

This design is generic and can be used with almost any
combination of graphics. For a simpler design, delete the
border. The line pattern can also be drawn so that the lines
are closer together or further apart.

Alternate Graphics
For **MR SUN** use **#19**
For **POT** use **COOKING** (GL2)
For **MAIL** use **PAINT** (GL1) or **TOOLS** (GL2–IBM/GL1)

Sign 1/FAMILY INFORMATION

What you need:

What you do:

SIGN; DYO; BORDER:LATTICE;
GRAPHIC:OTHER(MOD:HOUSE, page
187); SIZE:SM; LAYOUT;CUSTOM(2);
FONT:TYPEWRITER;
MESSAGE:L3(C,□)text,L4(C,■,CH
SIZE:L)text, L6-L13(C,■)text; CENTER:N;
PRINT

Design Notes:

This design works well for any kind of announcement.
Try typing a letter or note to a friend using the sign mode and
typewriter font.

Alternate Graphics
For **HOUSE** use **#31** or **CREST** (GL2) or **REMEMBER**
(GL3 – IBM/GL2)

Sign 2/CHILD'S ROOM

What you need:

What you do:

SIGN; DYO; BORDER:NO;
GRAPHIC:BY#(36); SIZE:LG;
FONT:NEWS; MESSAGE:L1(C,■,CH
SIZE:L)text; L10(IBM/L9)(1 space
between all letters) (C,■)text;
CENTER:N; Mark your original print
starting point and then PRINT

*To add STOP graphic and additional
message, roll back paper to original
print starting point.*

LETTER TOP; DYO;
GRAPHIC:OTHER(GL3:STOP –
IBM/GL2); POSITION:SIX; FONT:NO;
ADDRESS:NO; LINE:N

LETTER BOTTOM;
GRAPHIC:OTHER(GL3:STOP –
IBM/GL2); POSITION:BOTH; FONT:NO;
ADDRESS:L1-L3(C)text; LINE:N; PRINT

Design Notes:

A fiercer or more gracious message can be delivered through
the use of other graphics. A child's name (e.g. JANE'S) can be
used to replace the STOP signs at the top. An overall pattern
behind the sign can add further flavor.

Alternate Text
For STOP use child's name
For message at bottom use SERIOUS CONSEQUENCES or
NO GIRLS(BOYS) ALLOWED

Alternate Graphics
Gracious: For #36 use #46 or **MIME** (GL1)
Fierce: For #36 use #26 or **ROBOT** (GL1)

Sign 3/ LEMONADE STAND

What you need:

What you do:

SIGN; DYO; BORDER:NO;
GRAPHIC:OTHER(GL3:DRINK–
IBM/#100); SIZE:SM; LAYOUT:TILED;
FONT:NO; Mark your print starting point
and then PRINT (Note: Turn off printer
as soon as first row of the graphic prints
and then press ESC (←/Comm.) to exit
print mode.)

*To add MR SUN graphic and lemonade
message, roll back paper to original
print starting point.*

SIGN; DYO; BORDER:NO;
GRAPHIC:OTHER(GL3:MR SUN –
IBM/GL2); SIZE:MED;
LAYOUT:CUSTOM(3);FONT:STENCIL;
MESSAGE:L2,L12(C,■,CH SIZE:L)text,
L14(C,■)text; CENTER:Y; PRINT

*To add HOT graphic, roll back paper to
original print starting point.*

SIGN; DYO; BORDER:NO;
GRAPHIC:OTHER(GL3:HOT – IBM/GL2);
SIZE:SM; LAYOUT:CUSTOM(6,8);
FONT:NO; PRINT

*To add message at bottom, roll back
paper to original print starting point.*

LETTER TOP; DYO; GRAPHIC:NO;
FONT:NO; ADDRESS:NO; LINE:N

LETTER BOTTOM; GRAPHIC:NO;
FONT:BLOCK; NAME(C,□):text;
ADDRESS:L1,L2(C)text; LINE:Y; PRINT

Design Notes:

You may want to replace MR SUN graphic with DRINK graphic
if hot weather is not a strong selling point.

Alternate Graphics
For **MR SUN** use **#19** or **PARK** (GL1)

Sign 4/ REFRIGERATOR

What you need:

What you do:

SIGN; DYO; BORDER:NO;
GRAPHIC:OTHER(GL1:PLATE); SIZE:LG;
FONT:TECH; MESSAGE:L1(C,■,CH
SIZE:L)text, L10(IBM/L9)(C,■)text;
CENTER:N; Mark your original print
starting point and then PRINT

*To add ice cream cone graphic, roll back
paper to original starting point.*

SIGN; DYO; BORDER:NO;
GRAPHIC:BY#(14); SIZE:SM;
LAYOUT:CUSTOM(7); FONT:NO; PRINT

*To add NO graphic, roll back paper to
original print starting point.*

SIGN; DYO; BORDER:NO;
GRAPHIC:OTHER(GL3:NO – IBM/GL2);
SIZE:SM; LAYOUT:CUSTOM(7);
FONT:NO; PRINT

Design Notes:

Although not as powerful a statement without the "NO FOOD"
combined graphic, your reminder can be created using the
large PLATE graphic only. Alternate graphics for the ice cream
cone are tricky because few are smaller than the NO graphic.

Alternate Graphics
For **PLATE** use #14 or #50
If seeing food only makes you hungrier, use #18 or
REMEMBER (GL3 – IBM/GL2)!

Stencil

What you need:

What you do: ✂

BANNER; FONT:STENCIL;
MESSAGE:(S)text; GRAPHIC:NO; PRIN

*Cut out letters and then use your stenc
with paint, crayons or markers.*

Design Notes:

Print Shop banners make great stencils! Shown here is a
sample clubhouse sign. For a more durable stencil, attach your
printed banner to lightweight cardboard with rubber cement
or spray mount and then cut out your letters. To make sure
your letter placement is accurate, first trace your message in
pencil on the surface to be stenciled. Check your layout and
then, leaving your stencil in place, transfer your message.
Spray paint works best with large stencils.

Banner 1/BIRTHDAY

What you need:

What you do:

BANNER; FONT:PARTY;
MESSAGE:(S)text;
GRAPHIC:OTHER(MOD:BIRTHDAY
CAKE, page 176);
POSITION:BOTH;PRINT

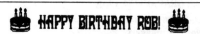

Design Notes:

Customize your banner with art you have modified for a more
personal look. The simpler and bolder the graphic, the more
readable it will be when printed in the large banner size.

Alternate Graphics
For **BIRTHDAY CAKE** use #1 or #2 or **PARTY2** (GL1)

Banner 2/ BIRTHDAY (STACKED)

What you need:

What you do:

For HAPPY BIRTHDAY banner:
BANNER; FONT:BLOCK; MESSAGE
(1 space between all letters, 2 spaces
between words)(S)text; GRAPHIC:NO;
PRINT
For NAME banner:
BANNER; FONT:ALEXIA;
MESSAGE(S)text; GRAPHIC:NO;PRINT
For DATE banner:
BANNER; FONT:BLOCK;
MESSAGE(S)text; GRAPHIC:NO;PRINT
*For top and bottom BIRTHDAY CAKE
banners:*
BANNER; FONT:NO;
GRAPHIC:OTHER(MOD:BIRTHDAY
CAKE, page 176); POSITION:BEFORE;
PRINT and then continue to PRINT until
you have printed the number of graphics
needed to frame your message.
*Stack banners and attach with tape on
back.*

Hints:

Several banners can also be attached at
the side or "chained" to make a very long
banner.

Design Notes:

Stacked banners can be used to create an "oversized sign." To
center the lines of your message after your individual banners
are printed, count the number of sheets used in your longest
banner. Then, use that same number of blank sheets to paste
up each of your shorter banners. Simply center the shorter
banner onto the blank sheets and attach with tape or glue.
Your individual banners all become the same length and
can easily be stacked as shown. By choosing a graphic and
then choosing to print repeatedly you can create a banner
to "frame" your sign.

Card 1/INVITATION

What you need:

What you do:

CARD FRONT; DYO; BORDER:THIN;
GRAPHIC:NO; FONT:BLOCK;
MESSAGE:L1,L3(C,■,CH SIZE:L)text;
CENTER:N

CARD INSIDE; BORDER:BEAD;
GRAPHIC:BY#(52–IBM/122); SIZE:SM;
LAYOUT:TILED; FONT:PARTY;
MESSAGE:L1(1 space between all letters,
2 spaces between words)(C,■)text,
L2(C,■,CH SIZE:L)text,L7-L10(IBM/L6-
L9)(L,■)text; CENTER:Y; Mark your
original print starting point and then
PRINT

*To add BEACH graphic, roll back paper
to approximately 2⅛ inches below your
original print starting point.*

CARD FRONT; DYO; BORDER:NO;
GRAPHIC:OTHER(GL2:BEACH);
SIZE:SM; LAYOUT:TILED; FONT:NO

*Select NO for all CARD INSIDE choices
and then PRINT. (Note: Turn off printer
when fourth row of BEACH graphic
prints and then press ESC (←/Comm.)
to escape print mode.)*

*To add FISH graphic, roll back paper to
original print starting point.*

CARD FRONT; DYO; BORDER:NO;
GRAPHIC:NO; FONT:NO

CARD INSIDE; BORDER:NO;
GRAPHIC:OTHER(GL1:FISH2);
SIZE:MED; LAYOUT:CUSTOM(3);
FONT:NO; PRINT

Card Front

Card Inside

Design Notes:

For a simpler design, delete the background pattern of the
Card Inside and print the graphic and text at the same time.
Try using other graphics tiled halfway down the page for
different purposes.

Alternate Graphics
For **BEACH** use **KEYBOARD** (GL2) or **SHELL** (GL2)
or **SCORE** (GL2)
For **FISH2** use **MR SUN** (GL3 – IBM/GL2) or #19

Card 2/THANK YOU

What you need:

Card Front

Card Inside

What you do:

CARD FRONT; DYO; BORDER:DOUBLE;
GRAPHIC:OTHER(GL1:FLOWERS);
SIZE:SM; LAYOUT:TILED;
FONT:STENCIL; MESSAGE:L1(C,■,CH
SIZE:L)text; CENTER:N

CARD INSIDE; BORDER:HEART;
GRAPHIC:NO; FONT:PARTY;
MESSAGE:L1,L4-L6(C,■)text,L2(C,■,CH
SIZE:L)text,L9-L10(IBM/L8-
L9)(C,■)text; CENTER:Y; Mark your
original print starting point and then
PRINT

*To add BEAR graphic, roll back paper to
original print starting point.*

CARD FRONT; DYO; BORDER:NO;
GRAPHIC:OTHER(ORIG:BEAR, page
155); SIZE:LG; FONT:NO

*Select NO for all CARD INSIDE choices
and then PRINT.*

Hints:

Graphics printed over a patterned
background should have a lot of solid
black areas for better contrast.

Design Notes:

To simplify this card, print the BEAR without the background
pattern. If you aren't inclined to create the BEAR, use #43
instead.

Alternate Graphics
For **FLOWERS** use **#2** or **#56**(IBM/**#126**) or
#60(IBM/**#130**)
For **BEAR** use **#43** without background pattern

FOR
BEARING
WITH ME
THROUGH GOOD
AND BAD

LOVE,
CAROLYN

Favor/ COLORING SOUVENIR

What you need:

What you do:

SIGN; DYO;
BORDER:OTHER(HE:PUMPKINS);
GRAPHIC:OTHER(HE:FLIGHT); SIZE:SM;
LAYOUT:CUSTOM(1,3,11,13);
FONT:OTHER(HE:CREEPY);
MESSAGE:L2,L7(C,■)text; CENTER:Y;
Mark your original print starting point
and then PRINT

*To add HALLOWEEN graphic, roll back
paper to original print starting point.*
SIGN; DYO; BORDER:NO;
GRAPHIC:OTHER(HE:HALLOWEEN);
SIZE:MED; LAYOUT:CUSTOM(3);
FONT:NO; PRINT

*To add small text at top, roll back paper
to approximately 1¼ inches below
original print starting point.*
LETTER TOP; DYO; GRAPHIC:NO;
FONT:NO; ADDRESS:L1,L2(1 space
between all letters)(C)text,L3(C)text;
LINE:N

*Select NO for all LETTERHEAD BOTTOM
choices and then PRINT.*

*To add small text at bottom, roll back
paper to approximately 1¼ inches above
original print starting point.*
LETTER TOP; DYO; GRAPHIC:NO;
FONT:NO; ADDRESS:NO; LINE:N

LETTER BOTTOM; GRAPHIC:NO;
FONT:NO; ADDRESS:Ll-L3(C)text;
LINE:N; PRINT

Hints:

Note the personalization of souvenir with
guest's name. To save time, replace name
with a generic message such as THANKS
FOR (top line) COMING (bottom line).

Design Notes:

The Print Shop Holiday Edition is full of unique and fun
graphics, fonts and borders. Replace with other holiday
graphics appropriate to your occasion.

Game/ PIN-THE-TAIL

What you need:

What you do:
GRAPHIC EDITOR; GRAPHIC:BY#(45);
Erase the pig's tail and save your
modified graphic (NO TAIL) on a
personal disk
BANNER; FONT:NO;
GRAPHIC:OTHER(MOD:NO TAIL);
POSITION:BEFORE; PRINT

Hints:
If you don't have time to go into *The
Print Shop's* Graphic Editor to erase the
pig's tail, you can simply use white out
liquid or white artist's tape to delete the
tail.

Design Notes:
Use the banner mode to print out oversized graphics for party
games or decorations. For this game simply delete the pig's
tail. Then create a long curly tail out of yarn, paper or ribbon.
Run the ribbon over the blunt edge of a scissor to make a curl.
Alternate Graphics
For #45 use #44 or CAT (GL1) or ELEPHANT (GL1)

Nametags

What you need:

What you do: ✂

SIGN; DYO; BORDER:NO;
GRAPHIC:OTHER(GL1:PAINT); SIZE:SM;
LAYOUT:CUSTOM(1,3,6,8,11,13);
FONT:NO; Mark your original print
starting point and then PRINT

*Add each name separately. To add
name at top left, roll back paper to
approximately 2¼ inches below original
print starting point.*

LETTER TOP; DYO; GRAPHIC:NO;
FONT:NEWS; NAME:(L,■)text;
ADDRESS:NO; LINE:N

*Select NO for all LETTERHEAD BOTTOM
choices and then PRINT.*

*To add name at top right, roll back
paper to approximately 2¼ inches below
original print starting point.*

LETTER TOP; DYO; GRAPHIC:NO;
FONT:NEWS; NAME(R,■)text;
ADDRESS:NO; LINE:N

*Select NO for all LETTERHEAD BOTTOM
choices and then PRINT.*

*To add names in middle and at bottom,
follow same instructions shown above
for names at top. When ready to print,
roll back paper to the following
positions:*

Names in the middle – 6 inches below
original print starting point
Names at bottom – 9¾ inches below
original print starting point

*Fold your paper in half vertically to
measure and make your first cut. Then
stack your two halves, fold two times
and cut.*

JAN STEPHENS   WAYNE STEPHENS

RICK ODELL   MARK CARD

LESLIE WYANDT   KATRINA SOLLER

Design Notes:

Many Print Shop graphics work well as solitary graphics. For
nametags, look for graphics somewhere between a logo-like
look and decorative look. Several suggestions are listed below.

Alternate Graphics
For **PAINT** use **#24** or **#19** or **CHESS** (GL2) or **SEW** (GL2)
or **CAMERA** (GL2 – IBM/GL1)

Sign/ PIN-UP

What you need:

What you do:

SIGN; DYO; BORDER:NO;
GRAPHIC:OTHER(GL1:PARTY2);
SIZE:SM; LAYOUT:CUSTOM(1,3,11,12,13);
FONT:NEWS; MESSAGE:L1(1 space
between numbers)(C,3D,CH SIZE:L)text,
L3(1 space between all letters)(C,■)text,
L7,L8(IBM/L6,L7)(C,□)text; CENTER: N;
Mark you original print starting point and
then PRINT

*To add additional text and PARTY2
graphic in the middle, roll back paper to
approximately 4 inches below original
print starting point.*

LETTER TOP; DYO;
GRAPHIC:OTHER(GL1:PARTY2);
POSITION:BOTH; FONT:NEWS; NAME(1
space between all letters):(C,■)text;
ADDRESS:L1(1 space between all
letters/numbers, 2 spaces between
month, date and year)(C)text,
L2,L3(C)text; LINE:N

*Select NO for all LETTERHEAD BOTTOM
choices and then PRINT.*

Hints:

Save time by first printing multiple
copies in the sign mode. Then roll back
your pages and add nostalgic messages in
the letterhead mode, one at a time.

Design Notes:

Signs liven up a party! Try this idea – print the same sign
several times then use the letterhead mode to add various
tidbits from the past. Try coloring in your graphics with
brightly colored markers.

Alternate Graphics
For **PARTY2** use **#1** or **#16** or **BIRTHDAY CAKE** (MOD. ART,
page 176) or **WEDDING** (GL2 – IBM/GL1)

Wrapping Paper 1

What you need:

What you do:

SIGN; DYO; BORDER:NO;
GRAPHIC:BY#(2); SIZE:SM;
LAYOUT:CUSTOM(1,3,4,5,6,8,9,10,11,13);
FONT:PARTY(IBM/STARLET);
MESSAGE:L1,L5,L9(C,■,CH SIZE:L)text;
CENTER:N; PRINT

Hints:

For a larger sheet of wrapping paper,
tape together several 8½ x 11 sheets.

Design Notes:

Try a graphic that has a good amount of white space and color
in with multiple-colored markers. Or select your font in outline
and color in your text. For a long name use initials or select
graphics only in rows between the text. It's easy to change the
look of your wrapping paper by selecting different graphics.

Alternate Graphics
For CHILD: **#14**
For FORMAL LOOK: **GRID** (MOD. ART, page 210)
For ADULT look: **#25** or **#48**

Wrapping Paper 2

What you need:

What you do:

SIGN; DYO; BORDER:NO;
GRAPHIC:OTHER(GL3:BOUQUET –
IBM/GL2); LAYOUT:STAGGERED;
FONT:NO; Mark your original print
starting point and then PRINT

*To add stork graphic at top and middle,
roll back paper to approximately 1⅞
inches above original print starting
point.*

SIGN; DYO; BORDER:NO;
GRAPHIC:BY#(5);
LAYOUT:STAGGERED; FONT:NO; PRINT

*To add stork graphic at bottom, roll
paper to approximately 5¾ inches below
original print starting point.*

SIGN; DYO; BORDER:NO;
GRAPHIC:BY#(5);
LAYOUT:CUSTOM(4,5); FONT:NO; PRINT

Hints:

For a shorter sheet and fewer printings
cut off the last row of graphics.

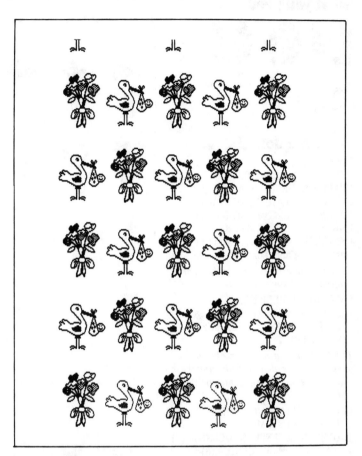

Design Notes:

Many graphics will complement one another in this staggered
pattern. Contrasting graphics (e.g. bold/detailed,
animate/inanimate) will work best. Try graphics with large
areas of white space and color in with markers.

Alternate Graphics
For HOUSE-WARMING: #19 and #31
For OLDER CHILD: #46 and **MOON** (GL1)

Alphabet Flash Cards

What you need:

(App/ Comm only)

What you do: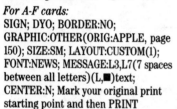

For A-F cards:
SIGN; DYO; BORDER:NO; GRAPHIC:OTHER(ORIG:APPLE, page 150); SIZE:SM; LAYOUT:CUSTOM(1); FONT:NEWS; MESSAGE:L3,L7(7 spaces between all letters)(L,■)text; CENTER:N; Mark your original print starting point and then PRINT

To add BEAR graphic, roll back paper to original print starting point.

SIGN; DYO; BORDER:NO; GRAPHIC:OTHER(ORIG:BEAR, page 155); SIZE:SM; LAYOUT:CUSTOM(2); FONT:NO; PRINT

To add all other graphics, make the same choices as above substituting the below graphics in the graphic positions indicated:

C: OTHER(GL1:CAT)/CUSTOM(3)
D: BY#(41)/CUSTOM(6)
E: OTHER(GL1:ELEPHANT)/CUSTOM(7)
F: OTHER(GL1:FISH)/CUSTOM(8)

For G-L cards
Follow the same steps as above substituting the following graphics in the positions indicated:
G:OTHER(GL1:GIRL)/CUSTOM(1);
H:OTHER(MOD:HOUSE, page 187)/CUSTOM(2);
I:OTHER (GL1:INDIAN)/CUSTOM(3);
J:OTHER(ORIG:JACK-IN-THE-BOX, page 167)/CUSTOM(6);K:OTHER(GL2:KEY–IBM/GL1)/CUSTOM(7);
L:BY#(18)/CUSTOM(8)

See next page for Graphic Suggestions for M-Z cards.

Design Notes:

Children love the classic alphabet card concept. Make your own cards with unique passes through the printer. Mount your cards on thin cardboard. For multiple copies, copy on a copier before cutting. Try printing letters on back. Handletter or use press type to save time.

Alternate Graphics
For **A:** AIRPLANE (GL1)
For **B:** #43 (bear) or BICYCLE (GL2)
For **J:** #7 (jack-o'-lantern)
For **H:** #2 (heart)

Alphabet Cards/ CONCENTRATION GAME

What you need:

(See Alphabet Flash Cards)

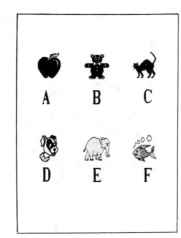

What you do:

(continued from previous page)

Graphic Suggestions for M-Z cards:
M:MONKEY(GL3 – IBM/GL2);
N:CHICK1(draw sticks over feet for
NEST)(GL1); O:OWL(GL1);
P:PIANO(#21); Q:PHAROH(draw crown
points for QUEEN)(GL2);
R:ROBOT(#36); S:SUNSHINE(#19);
T:TRAIN(#29); U:UMBRELLA(KEEP
DRY/GL3 – IBM/GL2);
V:INSTRUMENTS(red arrow to
VIOLIN)(GL2); W:WHALE(GL2 –
IBM/GL1); X:SKULL(delete bones and
draw box around skull for X-RAY)(#26);
Y:(add string for YO-YO)(#39);
Z:UNICORN(delete horn, draw in stripes
for ZEBRA)(GL3 – IBM/GL2)

Hints:

Older children are likely to get more out
of flash cards used in a game format.

Design Notes:

For a fun game of concentration, make 2 sets of alphabet cards
by copying your sheets on a copier. Hours of fun can be
supplied by this classic game. Lay the cards in rows face down.
Turn over two cards at a time and see if you have a match. If
you do, keep the pair and go again. If you don't, turn the cards
back over and try to remember the cards. The next player goes
and tries to make a match. The player who collects the most
cards wins. You can also play alone against the clock.

Any bold graphics will work. For this game of concentration,
you don't need to use alphabet cards. A simpler card with just
a picture or letter will work fine.

Coloring 1/ANIMALS

What you need:

What you do:

For CAT design:
SIGN; DYO; BORDER:DOUBLE;
GRAPHIC:BY#(42); SIZE:LG;
FONT:NEWS; MESSAGE(1 space between
all letters):L10(IBM/L9)(C,■)text;
CENTER:N; PRINT

For BUNNY design:
SIGN; DYO; BORDER:FLORAL;
GRAPHIC:BY#(46); SIZE:LG;
FONT:BLOCK; MESSAGE(1 space
between all letters):L14(IBM/L12)
(C,□)text; CENTER:N; PRINT

Design Notes:

Print Shop animals make terrific coloring sheets! Select
animals with a good amount of white space for better coloring
opportunities. For an additional challenge, omit one letter
from label at bottom for child to complete or use dashes and
let child fill in all letters. For group use, copy on a
copying machine.

Alternate Graphics
Use #44, #45, #47, #48 or GL1:CHICK, BUNNY,
ELEPHANT, PANDA, OWL, DOG, RACOON, ROOSTER,
FISH, BUTTERFLY, DINO (all three!)

Coloring 2/ASSORTED

What you need:

What you do:

SIGN; DYO; BORDER:THIN;
GRAPHIC:BY#(30); SIZE:MED;
LAYOUT:CUSTOM(3); FONT:STENCIL;
MESSAGE:L1,L2(L- indent 8 spaces,
■)text, L5(1 space between all
letters)(C,□,CH SIZE:L)text; CENTER:N;
Mark your original print starting point
and then PRINT

To add sun graphic, roll back paper to original print starting point.

SIGN; DYO; BORDER:NO;
GRAPHIC:BY#(19); SIZE:MED;
LAYOUT:CUSTOM(4); FONT:NO; PRINT

To add cat graphic, roll back paper to original print starting point.

SIGN; DYO; BORDER:NO;
GRAPHIC:BY#(42); SIZE:SM;
LAYOUT:CUSTOM(10,13); FONT:NO;
PRINT

Hints:

Choose graphics that are clean and open
for coloring. Copy on a copying machine
for group use. Simplify by using the same
graphic in several positions.

Design Notes:

Here are two additional coloring ideas.

Coloring 3/ PICTURE FRAME

What you need:

What you do:

SIGN; DYO; BORDER:WICKER;
GRAPHIC:BY#(2); SIZE:SM;
LAYOUT:CUSTOM(1,3,11,13); FONT:NEWS;
MESSAGE:L1,L2(C,■)text; CENTER:N;
PRINT

Design Notes:

A simple border turns a blank sheet of paper into a picture frame ready for a special picture. Kids may also enjoy pasting down photographs or magazine pictures.

Alternate Text
At top: ME, MY DOG, MY HOUSE, MY FAMILY, ANOTHER WORLD, SECRET PLACES, LOVE
At bottom: BY ME, child's initials

Alternate Graphics
For **WICKER** use **BEADS**
For #2 use graphic specific to title such as #20 for ANOTHER WORLD

Coloring 4/SAFETY

What you need:

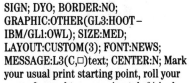

(App/ Comm only)

What you do:

SIGN; DYO; BORDER:NO;
GRAPHIC:OTHER(GL3:HOOT –
IBM/GL1:OWL); SIZE:MED;
LAYOUT:CUSTOM(3); FONT:NEWS;
MESSAGE:L3(C,□)text; CENTER:N; Mark
your usual print starting point, roll your
paper forward to approximately ¾ inch
below this point and then PRINT

*To add PHONE graphic, roll back paper
to approximately ¾ inch below usual
print starting point.*

SIGN; DYO; BORDER:NO;
GRAPHIC:OTHER(GL1:PHONE);
SIZE:SM; LAYOUT:CUSTOM(6);
FONT:NO;PRINT

*To add MAIL graphic, roll back paper to
approximately ¾ inch below usual print
starting point.*

SIGN; DYO; BORDER:NO;
GRAPHIC:OTHER(GL1:MAIL); SIZE:SM;
LAYOUT:CUSTOM(8); FONT:NO; PRINT

*To add name line and message at
bottom, roll back paper to usual print
starting point.*

LETTER TOP; DYO;
GRAPHIC:OTHER(GL1:WRITER);
POSITION:RIGHT; FONT:NEWS;
NAME:(L,■)text; ADDRESS:NO; LINE:N

LETTER BOTTOM; GRAPHIC:NO;
FONT:NEWS; NAME:(C,■)text;
ADDRESS:NO; LINE:N; PRINT

*To add phone number line, roll back
paper to approximately ¾ inch below
usual print starting point.*

LETTER TOP; DYO;
GRAPHIC:OTHER(GL1:WRITER);
POSITION:RIGHT; FONT:NEWS;
NAME:(L,■)text; ADDRESS:NO; LINE:N

MY NAME IS:
MY PHONE NUMBER IS:
MY ADDRESS IS:

BE WISE!

KNOW YOUR NAME AND ADDRESS!

Select NO for all LETTERHEAD BOTTOM
choices and then PRINT.

*To add address line, roll back paper to
approximately 1½ inches below usual
starting point.*

LETTER TOP; DYO;
GRAPHIC:OTHER(GL1:WRITER);
POSITION:RIGHT; FONT:NEWS;
NAME:(L,■)text; ADDRESS:NO; LINE:N

*Select NO for all LETTERHEAD BOTTOM
choices and then PRINT.*

Design Notes:

For a cleaner and simpler design, delete the two side graphics
and center text and print center graphic in large size.

Coloring 5/ALL ABOUT ME

What you need:

What you do: ✑

SIGN; DYO; BORDER:DOUBLE;
GRAPHIC:OTHER(GL1:GIRL);
SIZE:SM; LAYOUT:CUSTOM(11);
FONT:TYPEWRITER; MESSAGE:L1(1
space between all letters, 2 spaces
between words)(R,■)text, L5-
L10(L,■)text; CENTER:N; Mark your
original print starting point and then
PRINT

*To add THINKER graphic and text, roll
back paper to original print starting
point.*

SIGN; DYO; BORDER:NO;
GRAPHIC:OTHER(GL1:THINKER);
SIZE:SM; LAYOUT:CUSTOM(13);
FONT:NEWS; MESSAGE:L2(R,■,CH
SIZE:L)text; CENTER:N; PRINT

*To add WINNER graphic, roll back paper
to original print starting point.*

SIGN; DYO; BORDER:NO;
GRAPHIC:OTHER(GL1:WINNER);
SIZE:MED; LAYOUT:CUSTOM(1);
FONT:NO; PRINT (Note: Turn off printer
before graphic overlaps text), and then
press ESC (←/Comm.) to exit print
mode.)

Design Notes:

Children love activities involving fill-ins...especially about
themselves. Copy this design on a copying machine for
classroom, group or repeated use. Choose graphics that are
easy to color.

Alternate Graphics
For **GIRL** use **#47**
For **THINKER** use **#46**
For **WINNER** use **#44** or **WRITER** (GL1) or **DANCER** (GL1)

Creature Maker

What you need:

What you do:

SIGN; DYO; BORDER:NO;
GRAPHIC:OTHER(MOD:CREATURE
MAKER-1 (OR 2)), page 180); SIZE:LG;
FONT:NO; PRINT

Design Notes:

Print out and copy for hours of silly drawings. Erase the head,
legs or tail of any Print Shop animal. Just be sure to leave
enough room for a child to fill in his or her own creation. Print
in medium-size, staggered for an entire cast of characters.

Number Signs

What you need:

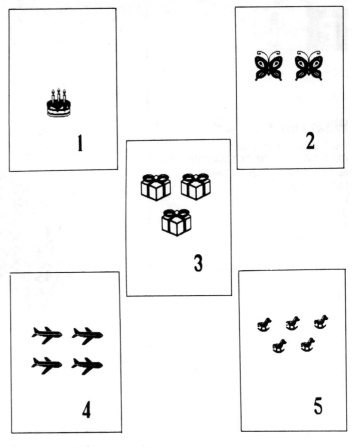

What you do:

For Number 1 sign:
SIGN; DYO; BORDER:NO;
GRAPHIC:OTHER(MOD:BIRTHDAY
CAKE, page 176); SIZE:MED;
LAYOUT:CUSTOM(3);FONT:NEWS;
MESSAGE:L9(IBM/L8)(R,■,CH
SIZE:L)text; CENTER:N; PRINT

For Number 2 sign:
SIGN; DYO; BORDER:NO;
GRAPHIC:OTHER(MOD:BUTTERFLY,
page 177); SIZE:MED;
LAYOUT:CUSTOM(1,2);FONT:NEWS;
MESSAGE:L9(IBM/L8)(R,■,CH
SIZE:L)text; CENTER:N; PRINT

For Number 3 sign:
SIGN; DYO; BORDER:NO;
GRAPHIC:OTHER(MOD:GIFT BOX,
page 185); SIZE:MED;
LAYOUT:CUSTOM(1,2,3); FONT:NEWS;
MESSAGE:L9(IBM/L8)(R,■,CH
SIZE:L)text; CENTER:N; PRINT

For Number 4 sign:
SIGN; DYO; BORDER:NO;
GRAPHIC:OTHER(MOD:PLANE, page
199); SIZE:MED; LAYOUT:CUSTOM(1,2);
FONT:NEWS;
MESSAGE:L9(IBM/L8)(R,■,CH
SIZE:L)text; CENTER:N; Mark your print
starting point and then PRINT

*To add additional PLANE graphics, roll
back paper to approximately 2½ inches
below original print starting point.*
SIGN; DYO; BORDER:NO;
GRAPHIC:OTHER(MOD:PLANE, page
199); SIZE:MED; LAYOUT:CUSTOM(1,2);
FONT:NO; PRINT

For Number 5 sign:
SIGN; DYO; BORDER:NO;
GRAPHIC:OTHER(MOD:ROCKER,
page 200); SIZE:SM;
LAYOUT:CUSTOM(1,2,3,4,5);
FONT:NEWS;
MESSAGE:L9(IBM/L8)(R,■,CH
SIZE: L)text; CENTER:N; PRINT

Design Notes:

Adding color with markers will make your number signs more
eye-catching. Note the need to choose graphics in the small
size for number groups above 4. Try copying the number signs
and letting children color them in. It's a great group activity.
For coloring, choose graphics with clean areas in which to color.

Paperdoll

What you need:

What you do:

SIGN; DYO; BORDER:NO;
GRAPHIC:OTHER(MOD: PAPERDOLL
CLOTHES-1, page 197); SIZE:MED;
LAYOUT:CUSTOM(2); FONT:NO; Mark
your original print starting point and
then PRINT

*To add PAPERDOLL graphic, roll back
paper to original print starting point.*
SIGN; DYO; BORDER:NO;
GRAPHIC:OTHER(MOD:PAPERDOLL,
page 196); SIZE:MED;
LAYOUT:CUSTOM(3); FONT:NO; PRINT

*To add PAPERDOLL CLOTHES graphic
at bottom, roll back paper to original
print starting point.*
SIGN; DYO; BORDER:NO;
GRAPHIC:OTHER(MOD:PAPERDOLL
CLOTHES-2, page 198); SIZE:MED;
LAYOUT:CUSTOM(4); FONT:NO; PRINT

Design Notes:

You may want to print the doll and clothes on separate sheets
of paper. For multiple copies, print in medium-size,
staggered. Color each outfit differently for a wardrobe with
variety! For a larger doll, print graphics in the large size.

Puzzle Game

What you need:

P

What you do: ✂ 📖

GRAPHIC EDITOR; GRAPHIC:BY#(45);
Draw GAME BOX shown on page 165
directly over the graphic. Save ANIMAL
IN BOX on disk.

SIGN; DYO; BORDER:NO;
GRAPHIC:OTHER(ANIMAL IN BOX);
SIZE:LG; FONT:NO; PRINT

Cut into four pieces.

Design Notes:

This jigsaw-like puzzle game can be created using any Print
Shop graphic. For a young child, select an item that is easy to
identify such as an animal or car. For a more challenging
puzzle divide the box into six or nine sections. Or choose a
design pattern such as #52 (IBM/#122) or #53 (IBM/#123).
For an alternate game, show child one puzzle piece and have
child match it to whole graphic on the graphic reference card.

Tic-Tac-Toe

What you need:

What you do:

SIGN; DYO; BORDER:NO;
GRAPHIC:OTHER(ORIG:TIC-TAC-TOE,
page 173), SIZE:SM;
LAYOUT:CUSTOM(1,2,3,4,5,6,7,8,9,10);
FONT:BLOCK(IBM/REPORTER);
MESSAGE:L13,L14(L,■)text; CENTER:N;
PRINT

Design Notes:

In addition to creating a Tic-Tac-Toe game, the graphic shown
here can be used as an interesting symbol or decorative graphic.
Try using it in tiled pattern on a letterhead (see page 173).

Travel Game

What you need:

What you do:

SIGN; DYO; BORDER:THIN;
GRAPHIC:OTHER(MOD:CAR, page 178);
SIZE:SM; LAYOUT:CUSTOM(1,3);
FONT:PARTY; MESSAGE:L1(C,■)text;
CENTER:N; Mark your original print
starting point and then PRINT

*To add state abbreviations, roll back
paper to original print starting point.*

SIGN; DYO; BORDER:NO; GRAPHIC:NO;
FONT:STENCIL; *MESSAGE:L1-L3,L5-
L14(3 spaces between states)(C,■)text,
L4(4 spaces between states)(C,■)text;
CENTER:N; PRINT

*To add additional text at top, roll back
paper to approximately 2 inches below
original print starting point.*

LETTER TOP; DYO; GRAPHIC:NO;
FONT:NEWS; NAME:(1 space between all
letters)(C,■)text; ADDRESS:NO; LINE:Y

*Select NO for all LETTERHEAD BOTTOM
choices and then PRINT.*

**(Note: The space between state
abbreviations varies depending on the
width of the letters in that row. To align
your columns, simply adjust spacing for
your arrangement. Most arrangements
work with either 3 or 4 spaces between
abbreviations.)*

		SPOT IT!		
		U S A		
WA	MT	OR	AK	WY
CA	NV	TX	CO	AZ
NM	ND	SD	MN	WI
NE	IA	IL	IN	MI
HI	OH	KS	MO	OK
AK	AR	LA	KY	WV
VA	TN	NC	SC	MS
AL	GA	FL	PA	MD
DE	NJ	CT	RI	NY
ID	MA	NH	VT	ME

Design Notes:

Copy sheets of this game for hours of travel fun. Match state
license plates on the road to your game sheet. Be the first
player to spot a state on your sheet and you've "captured" that
state. Only one player can "capture" each state. So work fast!
Use different colored crayons or pencils for each player to
circle a "captured" state (or mark the "captured" state
with an "X" or "O"). Mix up the abbreviations for a brand
new game.

Alternate Graphics
For **CAR** use **#28** or **#38**

Tri-Dot Game

What you need:

What you do:

SIGN; DYO; BORDER:NO;
GRAPHIC:OTHER(ORIG:DOTS,
page 161); SIZE:SM; LAYOUT:TILED;
FONT:NO; PRINT

Design Notes:

Skill and strategy are involved in this connect-the-dots game.
Each player takes a turn connecting two dots either
horizontally or vertically. Each time a player draws a line that
completes a box, the player "claims" the box by filling in
his/her initials and gets another turn. The player who "claims"
the most boxes wins.

Ad/EVENT

What you need:

What you do:

SIGN; DYO; BORDER:THIN;
GRAPHIC:BY#(24); SIZE:SM;
LAYOUT:CUSTOM(1,3,11,13); FONT:NEWS;
MESSAGE:L1-L3(C,■)text; CENTER:N;
Mark your original print starting point
and then PRINT

*To add drum graphic, roll back paper to
original print starting point.*

SIGN; DYO; BORDER:NO;
GRAPHIC:BY#(22); SIZE:SM;
LAYOUT:CUSTOM(6); FONT:NO; PRINT

*To add trumpet graphic, roll back paper
to original print starting point.*

SIGN; DYO; BORDER:NO;
GRAPHIC:BY#(23); SIZE:SM;
LAYOUT:CUSTOM(8); FONT:NO; PRINT

*To add text in middle, roll back paper to
approximately ½ inch above original
print starting point.*

SIGN; DYO; BORDER:NO; GRAPHIC:NO;
FONT:ALEXIA; MESSAGE:L5-
L7(C,■)text; CENTER:N; PRINT

*To add text at bottom, roll back paper to
approximately ½ inch above original
print starting point.*

LETTER TOP; DYO; GRAPHIC:NO;
FONT:NO; ADDRESS:NO; LINE:N

LETTER BOTTOM; GRAPHIC:NO;
FONT:NO; ADDRESS:L1-L3(C)text;
LINE:N; PRINT

Hints:

Leave plenty of white space around your
text for ads that are to be reduced in size
for publication. Ad layouts also make
excellent flyers or signs!

Design Notes:

Combine fonts, combine graphics, combine the sign and
letterhead modes—these tricks are easy to implement and
can add greatly to the impact of your design. Select graphics
appropriate to your message.

Alternate Graphics
For musical theme: **BAND** (GL2) or **SCORE** (GL2) or
INSTRUMENTS (GL2)

Badge

What you need:

What you do: ✂ 📄

GRAPHIC EDITOR;
GRAPHIC:OTHER(ORIG:TEMPLATE
BOX, page 172); Erase all tick marks
inside the box and save EMPTY BOX on
disk.

*To add EMPTY BOX graphic, mark your
usual print starting point and roll your
paper forward to approximately 1¼
inches below this point.*

SIGN; DYO; BORDER:NO;
GRAPHIC:OTHER(ORIG:EMPTY BOX);
SIZE:MED; LAYOUT:CUSTOM(3);
FONT:NO; PRINT

*To add heart graphic, roll back paper to
approximately 1¼ inches below usual
print starting point.*

SIGN; DYO; BORDER:NO;
GRAPHIC:BY#(2); SIZE:SM;
LAYOUT:CUSTOM(7); FONT:NO; PRINT

*To add text, roll back paper to usual
print starting point.*

SIGN; DYO; BORDER:NO; GRAPHIC:NO;
FONT:BLOCK(IBM/REPORTER);
MESSAGE:L3(C,■) 13 dashes,
L4(C,■)text, L5(C,■) 13 dashes;
CENTER:N; PRINT

Hints:

A medium-sized graphic in custom(3)
position and a small-sized graphic in
custom(7) position fall in the same place
on the page. Together they can create an
interesting effect as shown here. Just be
sure to roll back your paper to the same
print starting point when adding your
second graphic.

Design Notes:

Print and cut and you're ready to pin this badge on the
recipient of honor. Make your text line any length you need,
but try to keep it short or stack your words on top of one
another. For multiple badges, leave the text area blank, copy
the badge on a copying machine and then add names or text
by hand.

Alternate Graphics
For **#2** use **#36** or **WINNER** (GL1) or **SWIMMER** (GL1) or
RUNNER (GL1) or **THUMBS UP** (GL3 – IBM/#74)

Banner

What you need:

What you do:

To create top banner:
BANNER; FONT:NEWS;
MESSAGE:(S)text; GRAPHIC:NO; PRINT

To create middle banner:
BANNER; FONT:RSVP; MESSAGE(1 space
between all letters):(S)text;
GRAPHIC:OTHER(GL1:FOOTBALL);
POSITION:BOTH; PRINT

To create bottom banner:
BANNER; FONT:NEWS; MESSAGE(1
space between number sign and number,
2 spaces after number):(S)text;
GRAPHIC:NO; PRINT

*Stack banners and attach with tape
on back.*

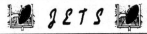

Design Notes:

Stacked banners can have tremendous impact as an "oversized" sign. Try dividing one long message onto 2, 3 or 4 stacked banners. To center the lines of your message after your individual banners are printed, count the number of sheets used in your longest banner. Then, use that same number of blank sheets to paste up each of your shorter banners. Simply center the shorter banner onto the blank sheets and attach with tape or glue. Your individual banners all become the same length and can easily be stacked as shown.

Chart/SEATING

What you need:

What you do:

SIGN; DYO; BORDER:NO;
GRAPHIC:OTHER(MOD:INITIALS,
page 195); SIZE:SM; LAYOUT:TILED;
FONT:STENCIL; MESSAGE:L2(C,■)text
CENTER:N; PRINT

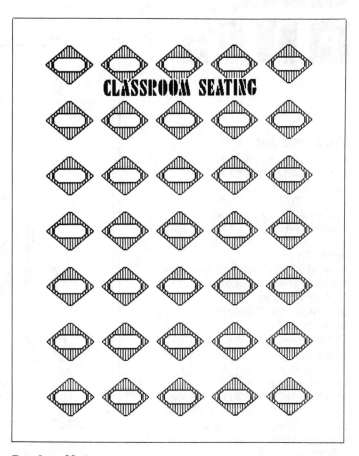

Design Notes:

For larger classes or for seating arrangements with additional
rows across, simply attach additional sheets with tape. Just
delete the text. This chart also works horizontally without the
text. Use chart as a quick reference for a substitute or
visiting teacher.

Flyer 1/BANQUET

What you need:

What you do:

SIGN; DYO; BORDER:DOUBLE;
GRAPHIC:OTHER(GL1:PLATE);
SIZE:MED; LAYOUT:CUSTOM(3);
FONT:PARTY(IBM/STARLET);
MESSAGE(1 space between all
letters):L7,L9(C,■)text; CENTER:N; Mark
your original print starting point and
then PRINT

*To add COFFEE graphic, roll back paper
to original print starting point.*
SIGN; DYO: BORDER:NO;
GRAPHIC:OTHER(GL3:COFFEE –
IBM/GL2); SIZE:SM;
LAYOUT:CUSTOM(2); FONT:NO; PRINT

*To add CHEF graphic, roll back paper to
original print starting point.*
SIGN; DYO; BORDER:NO;
GRAPHIC:OTHER(GL1:CHEF); SIZE:SM;
LAYOUT:CUSTOM(1,3); FONT:NO; PRINT

*To add text at top, roll back paper to
approximately 2½ inches below original
print starting point.*
LETTER TOP; DYO; GRAPHIC:NO;
FONT:NO; ADDRESS:L1(C)text,L3(1
space between all letters)(C)text;
LINE:N

*Select NO for all LETTERHEAD BOTTOM
choices and then PRINT.*

*To add text at bottom, roll back paper to
approximately 8¾ inches below original
print starting point.*
LETTER TOP; DYO; GRAPHIC:NO;
FONT:NO; ADDRESS:L1,L3(C)text;
LINE:N

*Select NO for all LETTERHEAD BOTTOM
choices and then PRINT.*

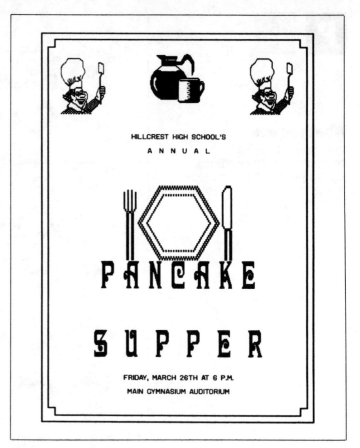

Design Notes:

Combining the letterhead and sign modes allows for headline
copy and lesser text to be used together to create an effective
flyer or sign. Notice in the letterhead mode that leaving a
blank line between text lines and extra spaces between letters
in words creates a more readable sign.

Alternate Graphics
For **PLATE** use **CHEF** (GL1) or **COOKING** (GL2)
For **CHEF** use **PLATE** (GL1)

Flyer 2/MEETING

What you need:

(App/ Comm only)

What you do:

SIGN; DYO; BORDER:THIN;
GRAPHIC:OTHER(GL3:THUMBS UP –
IBM/#74); SIZE:MED;
LAYOUT:CUSTOM(1); FONT:NEWS;
MESSAGE(1 space between all
letters):L7(IBM/L6)(C,■)text;
CENTER:N; Mark your original print
starting point and then PRINT

*To add THUMBS DOWN graphic and text
in middle, roll back paper to original
print starting point.*

SIGN; DYO; BORDER:NO;
GRAPHIC:OTHER(GL3:THUMBS DOWN –
IBM/#75); SIZE:MED;
LAYOUT:CUSTOM(5); FONT:RSVP;
MESSAGE(1 space between all
letters):L4(C,■)text; CENTER:Y; PRINT

*To add text at top, roll back paper to
approximately 3½ inches below original
print starting point.*

LETTER TOP; DYO; GRAPHIC:NO;
FONT:NO; ADDRESS:L1(C)text, L3(1
space between all letters)(C)text;
LINE:N

*Select NO for all LETTERHEAD BOTTOM
choices and then PRINT.*

*To add text at bottom, roll back paper to
approximately 9¼ inches below original
print starting point.*

LETTER TOP; DYO; GRAPHIC:NO;
FONT:NO; ADDRESS:L1(C)text; LINE:N

*Select NO for all LETTERHEAD BOTTOM
choices and then PRINT.*

Hints:

For greater interest and readability in the
letterhead mode, leave a blank line
between the first and last address lines
and leave spaces between the letters of
your words.

Design Notes:

Some messages are best communicated by a simple, yet strong
image. Look for "idea" graphics such as THUMBS UP and
THUMBS DOWN to deliver a strong statement. Mix fonts for
greater interest; combine sign and letterhead modes for
greater versatility.

Flyer 3/EVENT

What you need:

P 2 ³/1 (IBM)

What you do:

SIGN; DYO; BORDER:LATTICE;
GRAPHIC:OTHER(GL2:KEY – IBM/GL1);
SIZE:SM; LAYOUT:CUSTOM(1,2,3);
FONT:BLOCK(IBM/STENCIL);
MESSAGE:L4(C,☐,CH SIZE:L)text,
L8,L10(1 space between all
letters)(C,3D,CH SIZE:L)text;
CENTER:N; Mark your original print
starting point and then PRINT

*To add MR SUN graphic, roll back paper
to original print starting point.*

SIGN; DYO; BORDER:NO;
GRAPHIC:OTHER(GL3:MR SUN –
IBM/GL2); SIZE:SM;
LAYOUT:CUSTOM(11,13);
FONT:NO; PRINT

*To add text at bottom, roll back paper to
approximately 1⅛ inches above original
print starting point.*

LETTER TOP; DYO; GRAPHIC:NO;
FONT:NO; ADDRESS:NO; LINE:N

LETTER BOTTOM; GRAPHIC:NO;
FONT:NO; ADDRESS:L1-L3(C)text;
LINE:N

Design Notes:

The 3-D font style is effective for short messages. Combining
font styles is eye-catching for flyers. Multiple graphics are also
effective for decoration and greater communication. For use
as a sign, color in the outline font with a brightly colored
marker. You may want to color in some of the graphics as well.

Alternate Graphics
For **KEY** use **THUMBS UP** (GL3 – IBM/#74) or **STOP**
(GL3 – IBM/2) or **INSTRUMENTS**(GL2)
For **MR SUN** use #28

Letterhead 1/SCHOOL

What you need:

MONTESSORI SCHOOL

JIM BELEW, PRINCIPAL
3211 SUMMERSET DRIVE
SEATTLE, WASHINGTON 67643

What you do:

LETTER TOP; DYO;
GRAPHIC:OTHER(MOD:SCHOOL, page
201); POSITION:RIGHT; FONT:BLOCK;
NAME(1 space between all letters, 2
spaces between words):(L,■)text;
ADDRESS:NO; LINE:N

LETTER BOTTOM; GRAPHIC:NO;
FONT:NO; ADDRESS:L1-L3(L)text;
LINE:N; PRINT

Design Notes:

For many designs think "less is more." A simple design with
text at bottom can be very effective. Letter spacing can also
contribute to an open and clean look. To add prominence to
person's name, move name to address line 3 at top. Then move
up address 1 line at bottom. If desired, add phone number to
line 3.

Alternate Graphics
For **SCHOOL** use **#31** or **KIDS** (GL1) or **READER** (GL1)

Letterhead 2/CLUB

What you need:

What you do:

LETTER TOP; DYO;
GRAPHIC:OTHER(ORIG:FACES, page
162); POSITION:BOTH; FONT:BLOCK;
NAME (1 space between all letters,
3 spaces between words)(C,■)text;
ADDRESS:L2,L3(C)text; LINE:Y

LETTER BOTTOM; GRAPHIC:NO;
FONT:NO; ADDRESS:L1(L)text;
LINE:Y; PRINT

DEBATE   CLUB

HEAD TO HEAD
ON ISSUES THAT MATTER

THOMAS JEFFERSON HIGH SCHOOL

Design Notes:

For an alternate design, add motto and address to bottom of
letterhead and move school name to address line 1 at top. Here
a smaller font was selected to complement the strong graphic.
The font is softened by spacing out the letters and words.

Alternate Graphics
For **FACES** use **#39** or **SCALE** (MOD. ART, page 190)

Letterhead 3/CLUB

What you need:

What you do:

LETTER TOP; DYO;
GRAPHIC:OTHER(ORIG:BOAT,
page 157); POSITION:TILED; FONT:NO;
ADDRESS:NO' LINE:N
LETTER BOTTOM; GRAPHIC:NO;
FONT:RSVP; NAME:(R,■)text;
ADDRESS:L1-L3(R)text; LINE:N; PRINT

MARINA DEL REY BOAT CLUB
104 VENUS STREET
MARINA DEL REY, CA 78543
000-000-0000

Design Notes:

Graphics that fill the template box create new patterns in a
tiled layout. The stripes of this graphic create a particularly
interesting pattern. You may want to create your own original
graphics using a variety of striped patterns.

Alternate Graphics
For **BOAT** USE **#51** (IBM/#121) or **#54** (IBM/#124) or
FISHTILE (GL1) or **ISLAND** (GL1)

Letterhead 4/CLUB

What you need:

THE OWL TENNIS CLUB
14 ORCHID ST.
SANTA CRUZ, CA. 97665

JACKIE WHITING
PRESIDENT

What you do:

LETTER TOP; DYO;
GRAPHIC:OTHER(ORIG:OWL, page 170);
POSITION:LEFT; FONT:STENCIL;
NAME:(R,■)text;
ADDRESS:L1,L2(R)text; LINE:Y

Select NO for all LETTERHEAD BOTTOM choices. Mark your usual print starting point, roll paper forward to approximately ½ inch below this point and then PRINT.

To add name and title, roll back paper to approximately 1¾ inches below usual print starting point.

LETTER TOP; DYO; GRAPHIC:NO;
FONT:NO; ADDRESS:L1,L2(R)text;
LINE:N

Select NO for all LETTERHEAD BOTTOM choices and then PRINT.

Hints:

Look at the handbook ideas for simplifying Print Shop graphics or creating bold new ones in the New and Modified Art section. Many are ideal for creating professional looking letterheads.

Design Notes:

A second pass through the printer allows you the flexibility to add your name below the address line as shown in this design. Another idea: put your motto above the line and your address below. Choose a graphic appropriate to your needs. Some bold graphics that work well as "stand alones" are listed below.

Alternate Graphics

For **OWL** use **HOUSE** (MOD. ART, page 187) or **CAR** (MOD. ART, page 178) or **DOLLAR** (MOD. ART, page 207) or **BOAT** (ORIG. ART, page 157) or **ART** (GL1)

Masthead/NEWSPAPER

What you need:

What you do:

LETTER TOP; DYO; GRAPHIC:BY#(23);
POSITION:SIX; FONT:NO; ADDRESS:NO;
LINE:N

Select NO for all LETTERHEAD BOTTOM choices. Mark your original print starting point and then PRINT.

To add school name and address, roll back paper to approximately 1 inch below original starting point.

LETTER TOP; DYO; GRAPHIC:NO;
FONT:NO; ADDRESS:L1-L3(C)text;
LINE:Y

Select NO for all LETTERHEAD BOTTOM choices and then PRINT.

To add newsletter name and 2 large trumpets, roll back paper to original print starting point.

SIGN;DYO; BORDER:NO;
GRAPHIC:BY#(23); SIZE:SM;
LAYOUT:CUSTOM(1,3); FONT:STENCIL;
MESSAGE:L1(C,3D)text; CENTER:N;
PRINT

Hints:

Mastheads work best with a line separating them from the area in which the body of the text will be added.

Design Notes:

You can use Print Shop generated graphics and type for reproducible final art. You may want to take your masthead to a local printer to get professionally printed multiple copies for pasting up your type. Or you can print enough copies on your printer to paste up your newsletters and simply copy the issues on a copying machine. You may want to substitute a motto for the name and address. Use a graphic appropriate to your image.

Alternate Graphics
For **#23** use **#21** or **#35** or **MIME** (GL1) or **SOCCER** (GL2–IBM/GL1)

Program Cover/RECITAL

What you need:

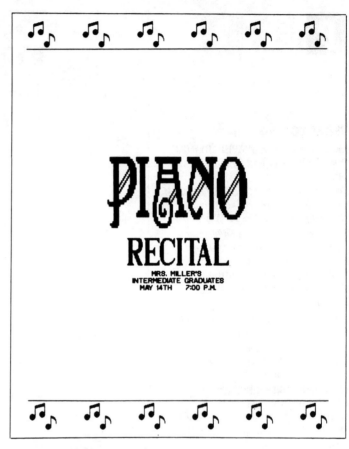

What you do:

LETTER TOP; DYO; GRAPHIC:BY#(24);
POSITION:SIX; FONT:NO; ADDRESS:NO;
LINE:Y

LETTER BOTTOM; GRAPHIC:BY#(24);
POSITION:SIX; FONT:NO; ADDRESS:NO;
LINE:Y; Mark your original print starting
point and then PRINT

*To add first line of text in middle,
roll back paper to original print
starting point.*

SIGN; DYO; BORDER:NO; GRAPHIC:NO;
FONT:ALEXIA; MESSAGE:L3(C,■,CH
SIZE:L)text; CENTER:N; PRINT

*To add second line of text in middle,
roll back paper to original print
starting point.*

SIGN; DYO; BORDER:NO; GRAPHIC:NO;
FONT:NEWS(IBM/STARLET);
MESSAGE:L6(C,■)text;
CENTER:N; PRINT

*To add text at bottom, roll back paper to
approximately 6¼ inches below original
print starting point.*

LETTER TOP; DYO; GRAPHIC:NO;
FONT:NO; ADDRESS:L1-L3(C)text;
LINE:N

*Select NO for all LETTERHEAD BOTTOM
choices and then PRINT.*

Hints:

For a simple, sophisticated look, use
letterhead mode graphic strips at top
and bottom to frame your layout.

Design Notes:

Piano, ballet, voice... any recital program cover can be
produced easily with *The Print Shop.* Mixing fonts allows you
to place emphasis where you need it. Combining the
letterhead and sign modes allows you to integrate descriptive
copy with a bold design.

Alternate Graphics
For #24 use **FLOWERS** (GL1) or **DANCER** (GL1) or **SCORE**
(GL2) or **KEYBOARD** (GL2)

Report Cover

What you need:

P **1** **2**

What you do:

SIGN; DYO; BORDER:THIN;
GRAPHIC:OTHER(GL2:MAP –
IBM/WORLD); SIZE:SM; LAYOUT:TILED;
FONT:NO; Mark your original print
starting point and then PRINT

*To add FLAG graphic and text, roll back
paper to original print starting point.*

SIGN; DYO; BORDER:NO;
GRAPHIC:OTHER(GL1:FLAG); SIZE:SM;
LAYOUT:CUSTOM(2); FONT:NEWS;
MESSAGE:L5-L10(C,■)text; CENTER:Y;
PRINT

*To add name at bottom, roll back paper
to approximately ⅜ inch above original
print starting point*

LETTER TOP; DYO; GRAPHIC:NO;
FONT:NO; ADDRESS:NO; LINE:N

LETTER BOTTOM; GRAPHIC:NO;
FONT:NEWS; NAME:(C)text;
ADDRESS:NO; LINE:N; PRINT

Design Notes:

Report cover designing is easy and effective using an overall
background pattern with bold text. There are many possible
layouts but a small graphic in the tiled pattern can be used
again and again to create an overall pattern that will hold your
design together. When choosing a graphic to print over your
background pattern, be sure to select one that is very dark.
Select graphics appropriate to your topic.

Sign/DIRECTIONAL

What you need:

What you do:

SIGN; DYO; BORDER:DOUBLE;
GRAPHIC:OTHER(ORIG:ARROW 2, page
152); SIZE:LG; FONT:NEWS; MESSAGE:
L1,L2,L9,L10(IBM/L1,L2,L8,L9)(C,■)
text; CENTER:N; PRINT

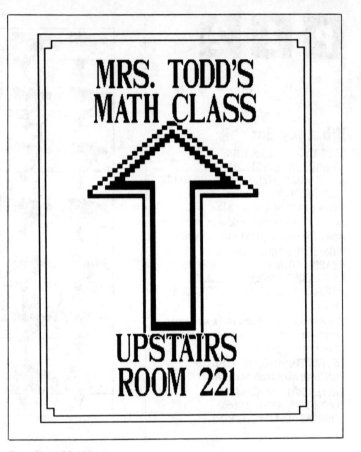

Design Notes:

A single, large arrow is effective for any kind of directional
sign. Color in outline of arrow with bright-colored markers
for added emphasis.

Tickets

What you need:

What you do:

SIGN; DYO; BORDER:NO;
GRAPHIC:OTHER(ORIG:FACES, page
162); SIZE:SM; LAYOUT:CUSTOM(1);
FONT:STENCIL;
MESSAGE:L1(R,■)text(add 3 spaces
after text),L2(R,■)text(add 6 spaces
after text); CENTER:N; Mark your
original print starting point and then
PRINT

To add additional tickets, roll back paper
to each of the following positions and
then choose PRINT:

Ticket 2 – 2½ inches below original print
starting point
Ticket 3 – 5 inches below original print
starting point
Ticket 4 – 7½ inches below original print
starting point

ADMIT ONE
$2.00

ADMIT ONE
$2.00

ADMIT ONE
$2.00

ADMIT ONE
$2.00

Design Notes:

Rolling back your paper and reprinting allows you to get 4
tickets on a sheet. Making multiple copies on a copier requires
one fourth the effort and one fourth the paper! To include
more detailed information specific to your event, use the
address lines of the letterhead mode. Choose a graphic
appropriate to your message. Review the New and Modified
Art section for graphics that are bold and simple.

Alternate Graphics
For **FACES** use **OWL** (ORIG. ART, page 170) or **BIRD** (ORIG.
ART, page 156) or **UNITED FIGURES** (MOD. ART, page 163)

Ad 1/ HELP WANTED

What you need:

What you do: ✂

LETTER TOP; DYO;
GRAPHIC:OTHER(GL2:INSTRUMENTS);
POSITION:LEFT; FONT:NEWS;
NAME:(C,■)text; ADDRESS:L1-
L3(C)text; LINE:N

LETTER BOTTOM; GRAPHIC:NO;
FONT:NO; ADDRESS:L1-L3(C)text;
LINE:N; PRINT

*Cut and paste up to fit your ad
specifications.*

Hints:

To create an ad:
1) Draw guidelines to represent your
ad size with light pencil on another
sheet of paper.
2) Cut your Print Shop type and art
into small enough pieces to work with
flexibility in pasting up your design.
3) Use spray mount or rubber cement
to mount your design. Line up with
a T-square or clear, plastic ruler.

PART-TIME SALES CLERK

EARN EXTRA DOLLARS DURING THE HOLIDAY SEASON.
MUSICAL INSTRUMENTS STORE IN NEIGHBORHOOD MALL.
PLEASANT WORKING CONDITIONS AND GOOD BENEFITS.

PREVIOUS EXPERIENCE HELPFUL BUT NOT NECESSARY.
CALL MR. HOLLINGSWORTH AT 000-0000 AFTER 2 P.M.
AN EQUAL OPPORTUNITY EMPLOYER.

Design Notes:

Print Shop art and type can be used quite successfully for
reproduction. This little ad was created from a letterhead
printed top and bottom that was cut and pasted. You may want
to be more elaborate and use several graphics. You can even
cut and use borders!

Alternate Graphics
Use descriptive graphic such as **#33** or **MECHANIC**
(GL2 – IBM/GL1) or generic graphic such as **CASHBOX**
(GL2 – IBM/GL1) or **DOLLAR** (MOD. ART, page 207)

Ad 2/PROMOTION

What you need:

What you do:

SIGN; DYO; BORDER:BEADS;
GRAPHIC:OTHER(GL1:SWIMMER);
SIZE:SM; LAYOUT:CUSTOM(1,3);
FONT:NEWS; MESSAGE:L1(C,■,CH
SIZE:L)text,L3,L4(C,■)text; CENTER:N;
Mark your original print starting point
and then PRINT

*To add MR SUN graphic and text in
middle, roll back paper to original print
starting point.*

SIGN; DYO; BORDER:NO;
GRAPHIC:OTHER(GL3:MR SUN–
IBM/GL2); SIZE:SM;
LAYOUT:CUSTOM(7);
FONT:BLOCK(IBM/REPORTER);
MESSAGE:L9-L12(C,■)text; CENTER:N;
PRINT

*To add text at bottom, roll back paper to
approximately ¾ inch above original
print starting point.*

LETTER TOP; DYO; GRAPHIC:NO;
FONT:NO; ADDRESS:NO; LINE:N

LETTER BOTTOM; GRAPHIC:NO;
FONT:NO; ADDRESS:L1,L2(C)text;
LINE:N; PRINT

Design Notes:

Reduce the number of printings by using the same graphic
in all 3 positions. If your print out requires more than a 50%
reduction to meet your ad specifications, try using a larger
font at the bottom such as typewriter in the sign mode. Just
reduce the sub-headline under your phone number to 2 lines.
Select a bold and simple center graphic. The corner graphics
can be more decorative.

Alternate Graphics
For **MR SUN** use #37 or #18
For **SWIMMER** use #32 or **DOLLAR** (GL2–IBM/GL1) or
DOLLAR (MOD. ART, page 207)

Ad 3/ OPENING RETAIL

What you need:

What you do:

SIGN; DYO; BORDER:STAR;
GRAPHIC:NO;
FONT:PARTY(IBM/STARLET);
MESSAGE:L1,L3(C,■,CH SIZE:L)text;
CENTER:N; Mark your original print
starting point and then PRINT

*To add text in middle, roll back paper to
original print starting point.*
SIGN; DYO; BORDER:NO; GRAPHIC:NO;
FONT:NEWS(IBM/STARLET);
MESSAGE:L5-L7(C,■)text; CENTER:N;
PRINT

*To add FOOTBALL graphic, roll back
paper to approximately 1 inch above
original print starting point.*
SIGN; DYO; BORDER:NO;
GRAPHIC:OTHER(GL1:FOOTBALL);
SIZE:SM; LAYOUT:CUSTOM(11);
FONT:NO; PRINT

*To add BASEBALL graphic, roll back
paper to approximately 1 inch above
original print starting point.*
SIGN; DYO; BORDER:NO;
GRAPHIC:OTHER(GL1:BASEBALL);
SIZE:SM; LAYOUT:CUSTOM(12);
FONT:NO; PRINT

*To add TENNIS graphic, roll back paper
to approximately 1 inch above original
print starting point.*
SIGN; DYO; BORDER:NO;
GRAPHIC:OTHER(GL1:TENNIS);
SIZE:SM; LAYOUT:CUSTOM(13);
FONT:NO; PRINT

*To add message at bottom, roll back
paper to approximately 1 inch above
original print starting point.*

LETTER TOP; DYO; GRAPHIC:NO;
FONT:NO; ADDRESS:NO; LINE:N
LETTER BOTTOM; GRAPHIC:NO;
FONT:NO; ADDRESS:L1-L3(C)text;
LINE:N; PRINT

Design Notes:

Print Shop designs can be used as final art for ads in
newspapers. The 8½ x 11 format reduces nicely to various sizes
of newspaper ads. Try different borders, fonts and graphics to
best reflect your image. Multiple graphics deliver more to your
message and make for a more interesting design.

Ad 4/PROMOTION

What you need:

What you do:

SIGN; DYO; BORDER:FLORAL;
GRAPHIC:OTHER(GL1:KIDS); SIZE:MED;
LAYOUT:CUSTOM(3); FONT:STENCIL;
MESSAGE:L1(C,■,CH SIZE:L)text,L3(2
spaces between all letters, 3 spaces
between words)(C,■)text,L4(C,□)text;
CENTER:N; Mark your original print
starting point and then PRINT

*To add text at bottom, roll back paper to
original print starting point.*

SIGN; DYO; BORDER:NO; GRAPHIC:NO;
FONT:BLOCK(IBM/REPORTER);
MESSAGE:L10,L12(IBM/L11,L13)(C,■)
text; L11,L13(IBM/L12,L14)(C,□)text;
CENTER:N; PRINT

Design Notes:

Combining fonts is particularly effective for designs that are
to be reduced in size for ad placement. This design works
equally well in the 8½ x 11 size as a flyer. Just copy on a
copying machine.

Alternate Graphics
For **KIDS** use **ROCKER** (GL1) or **ROCKER** (MOD. ART,
page 200) or **SCHOOL** (GL1)

Ad 5/Coupon

What you need:

P **1**

What you do:

SIGN; DYO; BORDER:FLORAL;
GRAPHIC:OTHER(GL1:FLOWERS);
SIZE:SM; LAYOUT:CUSTOM(6,7,8);
FONT:ALEXIA; MESSAGE:L1(C,■,CH
SIZE:L)text, L3(C,■)text; CENTER:N;
Mark your original print starting point
and then PRINT

*To add dotted line with text, roll back
paper to original print starting point.*
SIGN; DYO; BORDER:NO; GRAPHIC:NO;
FONT:NEWS;
MESSAGE:L7(IBM/L6)(C,■)dashes,
L8(IBM/L7)(2 asterisks on each side of
word) (C,■)text; CENTER:N; PRINT

*To add text at bottom, roll back paper to
approximately 1 inch above original
print starting point.*
LETTER TOP; DYO; GRAPHIC:NO;
FONT:NO; ADDRESS:NO; LINE:N
LETTER BOTTOM; GRAPHIC:NO;
FONT:TYPEWRITER; NAME:(C,■)text;
ADDRESS:L1-L3(C)text; LINE:N; PRINT

Hints:

Use in reduced size as an ad or use in
8½ x 11 size as a flyer. If your reduced ad
is of a different proportion delete the
border and use remaining design as is.

Design Notes:

By combining fonts and modes you can create an interesting
ad. Also, consider mixing Print Shop art and type with set type
or your own art. You can cut your design elements and paste
them up to create a camera ready mechanical for the printer.

Alternate Graphics
Select a decorative or logo-like graphic appropriate to your
message such as **#16** or **ART** (GL1) or **CAMERA**
(GL2 – IBM/GL1)

Banner Sale (Stacked)

What you need:

*(App/
Comm only)*

What you do:

To create middle banner:
BANNER; FONT:NEWS;
MESSAGE(S)text; GRAPHIC:NO; PRINT

To create bottom banner:
BANNER; FONT:RSVP; MESSAGE(S)text;
GRAPHIC:NO; PRINT

To create top banner:
BANNER; FONT:NO;
GRAPHIC:OTHER(GL3:YARDSALE –
IBM/#96); POSITION:BEFORE; PRINT
and then advance your paper
approximately 2 inches. Continue to
select the BEFORE position, print your
graphic and advance your paper 2 inches
until you have printed the number of
graphics needed to frame your message.

*Stack banners and attach with tape on
back.*

Design Notes:

Stacked banners can be used to create a huge, "oversized sign"
for store windows, hallways, or meeting room walls. By
choosing a graphic and then choosing to print repeatedly, you
can create a banner to decorate or "frame" your sign. To space
your graphics, advance your paper the same amount after
each graphic prints.

Alternate Graphics
Use graphics appropriate for your message such as #21 or
#24 (record store) or use generic graphics such as **DOLLAR**
(MOD. ART, page 207) or (GL2 – IBM/GL1) or **CASHBOX**
(GL2 – IBM/GL1)

Business Card 1

What you need:

What you do: ✂ ▱

For top card:
SIGN; DYO; BORDER:NO;
GRAPHIC:OTHER(GL1:FISH); SIZE:SM;
LAYOUT:CUSTOM(3); FONT:PARTY;
MESSAGE:L1,L2(L,■)text; CENTER:N;
Mark your original print starting point
and then PRINT

*To add name and title, roll back paper to
approximately 2¾ inches below original
print starting point.*
LETTER TOP; DYO; GRAPHIC:NO;
FONT:TYPEWRITER; NAME:(C,■)text;
ADDRESS:L1(C)text; LINE:N
*Select NO for all LETTERHEAD BOTTOM
choices and then PRINT.*

*To add address, roll back paper
approximately 4 inches below original
print starting point.*
LETTER TOP; DYO; GRAPHIC:NO;
FONT:NO; ADDRESS:L1-L3(C)text;
LINE:N
*Select NO for all LETTERHEAD BOTTOM
choices and then PRINT.*

For bottom card:
Make identical graphic and text choices
as shown above. For printings, roll back
paper to each of the following points:
Store Name: 5½ inches below original
print starting point
Your Name: 8¼ inches below original
print starting point
Address: 9 inches below original print
starting point
*Fold paper in half and then cut with
scissors.*

FREDDY'S FISH
AND PET SHOP

JOHN LINDSEY
ASSISTANT MANAGER

7800 HULEN STREET
BANGOR, MAINE 78654
000-000-0000

FREDDY'S FISH
AND PET SHOP

JOHN LINDSEY
ASSISTANT MANAGER

7800 HULEN STREET
BANGOR, MAINE 78654
000-000-0000

Design Notes:

Business cards don't have to be small! Make a statement with
an oversized card that is personalized and easy to update. You
may want to print on colored paper or photostat to a smaller
size and have a local print shop reproduce on a colored stock.

Alternate Graphics
For **FISH** use **DOLLAR** (MOD. ART, page 207) or **FIGURES**
(MOD. ART, page 208) or **BOAT** (ORIG. ART, page 157)

Business Card 2

What you need:

What you do:

For top card:
SIGN; DYO; BORDER:NO;
GRAPHIC:OTHER(MOD:CAR, page 178);
SIZE:SM; LAYOUT:CUSTOM(1);
FONT:NEWS; MESSAGE:L1(R,■)text;
CENTER:N; Mark your original print
starting point and then PRINT

*To add name and title, roll back paper to
approximately 2¼ inches below original
print starting point.*
LETTER TOP; DYO; GRAPHIC:NO;
FONT:NEWS; NAME:(C,■)text;
ADDRESS:L1(C)text; LINE:N

*Select NO for all LETTERHEAD BOTTOM
choices and then PRINT.*

*To add address, roll back paper to
approximately 3½ inches below original
print starting point.*
LETTER TOP; DYO; GRAPHIC:NO;
FONT:NO; ADDRESS:L1-L3(C)text;
LINE:N

*Select NO for all LETTERHEAD BOTTOM
choices and then PRINT.*

For bottom card:
Make identical graphic and text choices
as shown above. For printings, roll back
paper to each of the following points:
Company Name: 5½ inches below original
print starting point
Your Name: 7¾ inches below original
print starting point
Address: 9 inches below original print
starting point
*Fold paper in half and then cut with
scissors.*

Design Notes:

Business cards can be printed two to a page by rolling your
paper forward 5½ inches and starting your selection process
over. The New and Modified Art section of the handbook
provides lots of ideas as to how you can create a bold, clean,
personalized logo. Use the letterhead mode for longer text
messages on your business card.

Alternate Graphics
For **CAR** use **ART** (GL1) or **KEYBOARD** (GL2) or **MECHANIC**
(GL2)

Business Card 3

What you need:

What you do:

CARD FRONT; DYO; BORDER:WICKER;
GRAPHIC:OTHER(ORIG:SHEETS, page
171); SIZE:MED; LAYOUT:CUSTOM(1);
FONT:RSVP; MESSAGE(1 space between
all letters):L2(R,■)text; CENTER:N

*Make exact same choices for CARD
INSIDE. Mark your original print
starting point and then PRINT.*

*To add additional text, roll back paper
to original print starting point.*

CARD FRONT; DYO; BORDER:NO;
GRAPHIC:NO;
FONT:BLOCK(IBM/REPORTER);
MESSAGE:L5-L7(L,■)(space over to
center stacked names on top of one
another toward the right)text,
L9(C,■)text,L11-L13(C,■)text; CENTER:N

*Make exact same choices for CARD
INSIDE and then PRINT.*

*Cut out your cards using the borders as
your guide.*

Design Notes:

Business cards created in the greeting card mode have impact
due to their oversized nature. They're great as handouts on
store counters or at exhibits. For multiple original copies,
print lots of copies of your first pass, then roll back your paper
and add the remainder of your design to all copies at once by
choosing to print the same number of times. You can also use
your original as artwork for reproduction at a local print shop.
Choose a graphic appropriate for your profession or image.

Calendar/WEEKLY

What you need:

(App/ Comm only)

What you do:

CALENDAR; WEEKLY;
GRAPHIC:OTHER(GL3:DRIVER–
IBM/#65); POSITION:RIGHT;
YEAR:text; MONTH:text;
FONT:COMPANION(LOWER CASE);
MESSAGE:L1(■), L2(3D); FIRST
DAY:text; CENTER:text; BOTTOM:text;
PRINT

october
1988

MONDAY 10	CALL CPA
	11:00 IRVING SUPPLY EXECS/LUNCH
TUESDAY 11	10:00 BOB AND DAN
	2:30 THOMPSONS
	5:00 PICK UP GEORGE AT AIRPORT
	DELTA #32
WEDNESDAY 12	12 NOON BETTY GIBSON
	4342 ELM STREET
	4:00 WALTER'S MOTHER TO DOCTOR
THURSDAY 13	DAY OFF!!!!!!!!!!!!
	GOLF WITH ED!
FRIDAY 14	8:30 PICK UP EASTERN AUTO EXECS
	AT AIRPORT - UNITED #621
	2:00 SATURN PLAZA
SATURDAY 15	10:00 EYE DOCTOR APP'T
	1:45 SARAH WILSON AND WALTER
	TO GREEN CLUB OPENING
SUNDAY 16	O F F !

EXECUTIVE LIMOUSINE SERVICE WEEKLY APPOINTMENTS

Design Notes:

Using *The Print Shop* Companion offers an array of new
tools such as the ability to create calendars. Try further
personalizing your calendar with a company logo that is bold
and simple. Look for ideas in the New and Modified Art
section. Also note the monthly calendar in Home applications,
page 30.

Card 1/ANNOUNCEMENT

What you need:

*(App/
Comm only)*

What you do:

CARD FRONT; DYO; BORDER:THIN;
GRAPHIC:OTHER(GL3:GAVEL –
IBM/#92); SIZE:MED;
LAYOUT:CUSTOM(1,2,4,5);
FONT:NEWS(IBM/STARLET);
MESSAGE:L4-L7(C,■)text; CENTER:Y

CARD INSIDE; BORDER:THIN;
GRAPHIC:NO; FONT:NEWS
(IBM/STARLET); MESSAGE:L1-
L10(C,■)text; CENTER:Y; PRINT

Hints:

Try printing on colored computer paper.
Use a light colored paper such as cream,
yellow, or pale blue. You may also be able
to copy on to colored paper using a copying
machine. Check to see if paper of the right
thickness is available for your copier.

Card Front

Card Inside

THE PINEWOOD
SCHOOL
ANNOUNCES THE
APPOINTMENTS
OF JAMES LEE
AND
BILL FOXWORTH
AS NEW
PRINCIPAL AND
VICE PRINCIPAL.

Design Notes:

Often "less is more." A good design idea is as powerful on *The
Print Shop* as it is in any other design form. Here a simple
Card Front layout is complemented by an all type Card Inside.
Choose graphics appropriate for your message that are simple,
yet decorative.

Alternate Graphics

For **GAVEL** use **#16** or
CALCULATOR (GL2 – IBM/GL1) or
THUMBS UP (GL3 – IBM/#74)

Card 2/MOVED

What you need:

What you do:

CARD FRONT; DYO; BORDER:FLORAL;
GRAPHIC:OTHER(HE:ROOTS); SIZE:LG;
FONT:STENCIL;
MESSAGE:L1,L2,L13,L14(C,■)text;
CENTER:N
CARD INSIDE; BORDER:FLORAL;
GRAPHIC:OTHER(GL1:PARK); SIZE:SM;
LAYOUT:CUSTOM(11,12,13);
FONT:STENCIL; MESSAGE:L1-L5,L8-
L11(C,■)text; CENTER:N; PRINT

Card Front

Card Inside

Design Notes:

Use the quality of contrast in your designs. In designing a card, a large graphic with small type is effective for a single panel. A bold Card Front design contrasted with a delicate Card Inside design creates an interesting and professional looking layout.

Flyer 1/RECRUITMENT

What you need:

What you do:

SIGN; DYO; BORDER:THICK;
GRAPHIC:OTHER(GL1:BASEBALL);
SIZE:MED; LAYOUT:CUSTOM(3);
FONT:BLOCK; MESSAGE(1 space
between all letters):L1,L13(IBM/L11)
(C,■,CH SIZE:L)text; CENTER:N; Mark
your original print starting point and
then PRINT

*To add message near top, roll back
paper to approximately 2⅝ inches
below original print starting point.*

LETTER TOP; DYO; GRAPHIC:NO;
FONT:NO; ADDRESS:L1,L3(C)text,L2(1
space between all letters, 2 spaces
between words)(C)text; LINE:N

*Select NO for all LETTERHEAD BOTTOM
choices and then print.*

*To add message near bottom, roll back
paper to approximately 2⅞ inches
above original print starting point.*

LETTER TOP; DYO; GRAPHIC:NO;
FONT:NO; ADDRESS:NO; LINE:N

LETTER BOTTOM; GRAPHIC:NO;
FONT:NO; ADDRESS:L2,L3(C)text;
LINE:N; PRINT

Design Notes:

Any meeting or recruitment can be announced with a simple
flyer using one large graphic and text. Combine the letterhead
mode with the sign mode to add detailed information in a
small size. Choose graphics appropriate for your purpose.

Flyer 2/SERVICE

What you need:

What you do:

SIGN; DYO; BORDER:FLORAL;
GRAPHIC:OTHER(MOD:TREE, page 202);
SIZE:MED; LAYOUT:CUSTOM(3);
FONT:ALEXIA; MESSAGE(1 space
between all letters):L1,L7(C,■,CH
SIZE:L)text; CENTER:N; Mark your
original print starting point and then
PRINT

*To add additional text, roll back paper
to approximately 7 inches below
original print starting point.*

LETTER TOP; DYO; GRAPHIC:NO;
FONT:NO; ADDRESS:L1-L3(C)text;
LINE:N

*Select NO for all LETTERHEAD BOTTOM
choices and then PRINT.*

Design Notes:

An effective flyer can be created easily and quickly using a
large headline with one large graphic. For longer headline
words, delete the space between letters. Add secondary text
in a smaller size using the letterhead mode.

Alternate Graphics
For **FLORAL** border use **HEARTS**
For **TREE** use **PARK** (GL1) or **LEAF** (GL3 – IBM/GL2)

Flyer 3/SERVICE

What you need:

What you do:

SIGN; DYO; BORDER:DOUBLE;
GRAPHIC:OTHER(MOD:BUTTERFLY,
page 177); SIZE:SM;
LAYOUT:CUSTOM(1,3,7,11,13);
FONT:PARTY; MESSAGE(1 space
between all letters):L6,L8(C,■)text;
CENTER:Y; Mark your original print
starting point and then PRINT

*To add message at top, roll back paper to
approximately ½ inch below original
print starting point.*

LETTER TOP; DYO; GRAPHIC:NO;
FONT:NO; ADDRESS:L1,L2(C)text;
LINE:N

*Select NO for all LETTERHEAD BOTTOM
choices and then PRINT.*

*To add message at bottom, roll back
paper to approximately 1 inch above
original print starting point.*

LETTER TOP; DYO; GRAPHIC:NO;
FONT:NO; ADDRESS:NO; LINE:N

LETTER BOTTOM; GRAPHIC:NO;
FONT:NO; ADDRESS:L1-L3(C)text;
LINE:N; PRINT

Hints:

Check the Graphics Specifications
section to see if the graphic you choose
will work in the center position with the
type printing over it. Most graphics will
work satisfactorily.

Design Notes:

Combine the letterhead and sign modes in a variety
of different layouts for well designed flyers that are
easy to create.

Alternate Graphics
For **BUTTERFLY** use #11 or #31 or #49 or **HOME** (GL1)

Flyer 4/SERVICE

What you need:

(App/ Comm only)

What you do:

SIGN; DYO; BORDER:WICKER;
GRAPHIC:OTHER(GL3:RUSH–
IBM/#70); SIZE:SM;
LAYOUT:CUSTOM(6,7,8); FONT:NEWS;
MESSAGE:L4(C,■)text, L7(1 space
between all numbers)(C,■)text;
CENTER:Y; Mark your original print
starting point and then PRINT

*To add message at top and bottom, roll
back paper to original print starting
point.*

SIGN; DYO; BORDER:NO; GRAPHIC:NO;
FONT:STENCIL; MESSAGE:L1-L3,L12-
L14(C,■)text; CENTER:N; PRINT

Design Notes:

A repeat pattern of letters makes an interesting design
element. Substitute a message appropriate to your profession.
Also, use a graphic that reflects your business image.

Alternate Graphics
For **RUSH** use **POINTING FINGER** (MOD. ART, page 211)
or **PHONE** (GL1)

Interoffice 1/MEMO

What you need:

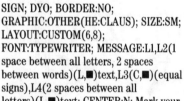

What you do:

SIGN; DYO; BORDER:NO;
GRAPHIC:OTHER(HE:CLAUS); SIZE:SM;
LAYOUT:CUSTOM(6,8);
FONT:TYPEWRITER; MESSAGE:L1,L2(1
space between all letters, 2 spaces
between words)(L,■)text,L3(C,■)(equal
signs),L4(2 spaces between all
letters)(L,■)text; CENTER:N; Mark your
original print starting point and then
PRINT

*To add alarm clock graphic, roll back
paper to original print starting point.*
SIGN; DYO; BORDER:NO;
GRAPHIC:BY#(37); SIZE:SM;
LAYOUT:CUSTOM(7); FONT:NO; PRINT

*To add single NOTE LINE at top, roll
back paper to original print starting
point.*
SIGN; DYO; BORDER:NO;
GRAPHIC:OTHER(ORIG:NOTE LINES,
page 169); SIZE:SM; LAYOUT:TILED:
FONT:NO; PRINT (NOTE: Turn off printer
after top line prints and then press ESC
(←/Comm.) to exit print mode.)

*To add NOTE LINES at bottom, roll back
paper to approximately 6¼ inches below
original print starting point.*
SIGN; DYO; BORDER:NO;
GRAPHIC:OTHER(ORIG:NOTE LINES,
page 169); FONT:NO; PRINT (NOTE: Turn
off printer after line at bottom of page
prints and then press ESC (←/Comm.) to
exit print mode.)

Design Notes:

If you need more lines, try the letterhead mode with
two graphics at top, one in each corner. Then simply
start printing the NOTE LINES higher on the page.

Alternate Graphics
Holiday: For **CLAUS** use **SANTA** (GL1) or **#9** or **#10**
Generic: For **CLAUS** use **#18** or **#38**

Interoffice 2/SIGN-OFF SHEET

What you need:

What you do:

SIGN; DYO; BORDER:THIN; GRAPHIC:OTHER(ORIG:BOOK, page 158); SIZE:MED; LAYOUT:CUSTOM(2); FONT:TECH; MESSAGE:L1(L,■)text; CENTER:N; Mark your original print starting point and then PRINT

To add second line of text, roll back paper to original print starting point.
SIGN; DYO; BORDER:NO; GRAPHIC:NÒ; FONT:NEWS; MESSAGE:L2(L,■)text; CENTER:N; PRINT

To add third line of text, roll back paper to original print starting point.
SIGN; DYO; BORDER:NO; GRAPHIC:NO; FONT:TYPEWRITER; MESSAGE:L5(L,■)(approximately 18 spaces between words)text; CENTER:N; PRINT

To add NOTE LINES, roll back paper to approximately 3¾ inches below original print starting point.
SIGN; DYO; BORDER:NO; GRAPHIC:OTHER(ORIG:NOTE LINES, page 169); SIZE:SM; LAYOUT:TILED; FONT:NO; PRINT (NOTE: Turn off printer after line at bottom prints and then press ESC (←/Comm.) to exit print mode.)

Design Notes:

To simplify, print all text in the same font. Stationery, memos and lists can all be created using the NOTE LINES graphic from the New Art section.

Alternate Graphics
For **BOOK** use **WRITER** (GL1) or **THUMBS UP** (GL3 – IBM/#74)

Letterhead 1/BUSINESS

What you need:

What you do:

LETTER TOP; DYO; GRAPHIC:NO;
FONT:TYPEWRITER; NAME:(L,■)text;
ADDRESS:L1(1 space between all letters,
2 spaces between words)(L)text; LINE:Y

LETTER BOTTOM; GRAPHIC:NO;
FONT:NO; ADDRESS:L1,L2(L)text;
LINE:N; PRINT

Hints:

Try letterhead designs without any
graphics for a more formal look.

JOHNSON, RICHARDS & NEWMAN
CERTIFIED   PUBLIC   ACCOUNTANTS

12600 MILITARY PARKWAY, SUITE 30
POMONA BEACH, FL 33142

Design Notes:

Typography, properly used, can create interesting designs.
For a different look, try positioning all your text at right or
in the center.

Letterhead 2/BUSINESS

What you need:

What you do:

LETTER TOP; DYO;
GRAPHIC:OTHER(UNITED FIGURES,
page 163); POSITION:TILED; FONT:NO;
ADDRESS:NO; LINE:N

LETTER BOTTOM; GRAPHIC:NO;
FONT:NO; ADDRESS:L2,L3(C)text;
LINE:N; Mark your original print starting
point and then PRINT

*To add message at top, roll back paper to
approximately ⅞ inch below original
print starting point.*

LETTER TOP; DYO; GRAPHIC:NO;
FONT:NEWS; NAME:(C,■)text;
ADDRESS:L2(C)text; LINE:Y

*Select no for all LETTERHEAD BOTTOM
choices and then PRINT.*

UNITED SHIPPING

HAND-TO-HAND DELIVERY

13711 OAK GROVE BOULEVARD
DALLAS, TEXAS 75229

Design Notes:

A repeat pattern design can be used to communicate a
concept or idea, or as a decorative element. Choose a graphic
that best conveys your message. Some graphics that work
well in repetition are listed below.

Alternate Graphics
For **UNITED FIGURES** use #18 or #24 or #34 or
COOKIES (GL1) or **DOLLAR** (GL2 – IBM/GL1) or
MEN (GL3 – IBM/GL2) or **WOMEN** (GL3 – IBM/GL2) or
THUMBS UP (GL3 – IBM/#74)

Letterhead 3/RETAIL

What you need:

What you do:

LETTER TOP; DYO; GRAPHIC:NO;
FONT:PARTY; NAME(1 space between
all letters, 2 spaces between
words):(C,■)text; ADDRESS:L1-
L3(C)text; LINE:N

LETTER BOTTOM;
GRAPHIC:OTHER(ORIG:HANGER, page
159); POSITION:TILED; FONT:NO;
ADDRESS:NO; LINE:Y; PRINT

THE CLOTHESHANGER
GREAT FASHIONS AT AN AFFORDABLE PRICE!
NORTHEAST MALL   MESQUITE, OREGON   98765
000-000-0000

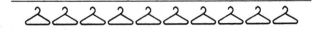

Design Notes:

Use one of the letterhead address lines for your sales pitch!
Choose a graphic appropriate for your line of work or message.

Letterhead 4/ RETAIL

What you need:

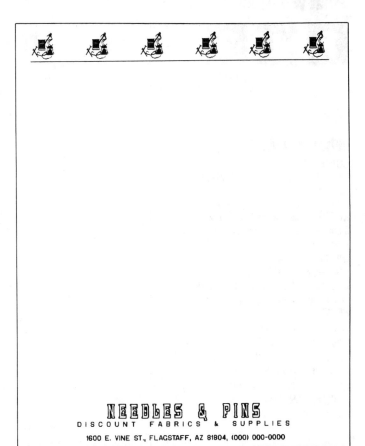

What you do:

LETTER TOP; DYO;
GRAPHIC:OTHER(GL2:SPOOL);
POSITION:SIX; FONT:NO; ADDRESS:NO;
LINE:Y

LETTER BOTTOM; GRAPHIC:NO;
FONT:NO; ADDRESS:L1(1 space between
all letters, 2 spaces between
words)(C)text,L3(C)text; Mark your
original print starting point and then
PRINT

*To add company name, roll back paper
to approximately ⅛ inch below original
print starting point.*

LETTER TOP; DYO; GRAPHIC:NO;
FONT:NO; ADDRESS:NO; LINE:N

LETTER BOTTOM; GRAPHIC:NO;
FONT:PARTY; NAME(1 space between
all letters, 2 spaces between
words)(C,□)text; LINE:N; PRINT

Hints:

Try letter spacing your descriptive line
for greater emphasis. Note the improved
readability when the middle address line
is skipped creating white space between
the descriptive line and address
information.

Design Notes:

By designing your letterhead with all text at the bottom, your
graphic will stand out and better communicate your message.
Many graphics are effective in the "six in a row" pattern.
Choose one appropriate to your line of work or image.

Letterhead 5/SMALL BUSINESS

What you need:

(App/ Comm only)

What you do:

LETTER TOP; DYO;
GRAPHIC:OTHER(GL3:THUMBS UP –
IBM/#74); POSITION:BOTH;
FONT:STENCIL; NAME:(C,■)text;
ADDRESS:L2(1 space between all letters,
2 spaces between words)(C)text; LINE:N

LETTER BOTTOM;
GRAPHIC:OTHER(GLI:PARK);
POSITION:RIGHT; FONT:NO;
ADDRESS:L2(C)text; LINE:Y; Mark your
original print starting point and then
PRINT

*To add rose graphic, roll back paper to
original print starting point.*

LETTER TOP; DYO; GRAPHIC:NO;
FONT:NO; ADDRESS:NO; LINE:N

LETTER BOTTOM; GRAPHIC:BY#(11);
POSITION:LEFT; FONT:NO;
ADDRESS:NO; LINE:N; PRINT

Design Notes:

A great deal of interest can be added to a business letterhead
simply by using multiple graphics. You can mix and match
appropriate graphics based on any theme that reflects your
image. For a bolder, more logo-like look, replace the PARK
graphic with the TREE graphic (MOD. ART, page 202).

Letterhead 6/ SMALL BUSINESS

What you need:

What you do:

GRAPHIC EDITOR;
GRAPHIC:OTHER(ORIG:ARROW1, page 151); Mark your original print starting point and then PRINT. Continue to select PRINT until arrow at bottom of page prints. (Note: Do not advance your paper each time.)

To add text, roll back paper to approximately ¼ inch above original print starting point.

LETTER TOP; DYO; GRAPHIC:NO; FONT:NO; ADDRESS:L1,L3(1 space between all letters, 2 spaces between words)(R)text; LINE:N

LETTER BOTTOM; GRAPHIC:NO; FONT:NO; ADDRESS:L1,L3(1 space between all letters, 2 spaces between words)(R)text; LINE:N; PRINT

Hints:

The Graphic Editor allows you to print graphics in the flush left position. By choosing PRINT repeatedly, you can print a column of the same graphic down the left side of the page. Or you can choose a different graphic each time.

Design Notes:

Flush right text works well with this flush left column of graphics. You may not want to space out your letters. Try this design with just your company name.

Alternate Graphics
Generic: For **ARROW 1** use **#18** or **#24** or **WRITER** (GL1)
Or choose graphics specific to your profession such as **PLUMBER** (GL2 – IBM/GL1) or **SEW** (GL2)

List 1/ DAILY TO DO

What you need:

What you do:

SIGN; DYO; BORDER:THIN;
GRAPHIC:OTHER(ORIG:BOOK, page
158); SIZE:SM; LAYOUT:CUSTOM(1,2,3);
FONT:TYPEWRITER(IBM/REPORTER);
MESSAGE(1 space between all letters, 2
spaces between words):L3(C,■)text;
CENTER:N; Mark your original print
starting point and then PRINT

*To add additional text, roll back paper
to original print starting point.*

SIGN; DYO; BORDER:NO; GRAPHIC:NO;
FONT:STENCIL; MESSAGE:L5(indent
approximately 6
spaces)(C,■)text,L14(C,■)text;
CENTER:N; PRINT

*To add NOTE LINES, roll back paper to
approximately 4½ inches below original
print starting point.*

SIGN; DYO; BORDER:NO;
GRAPHIC:OTHER(ORIG:NOTE LINES,
page 169); SIZE:SM; LAYOUT:TILED;
FONT:NO; PRINT (Note: Turn off printer
when NOTE LINES have printed
approximately 1½ inches from bottom to
avoid printing over text and then press
ESC (←/Comm.) to exit print mode.)

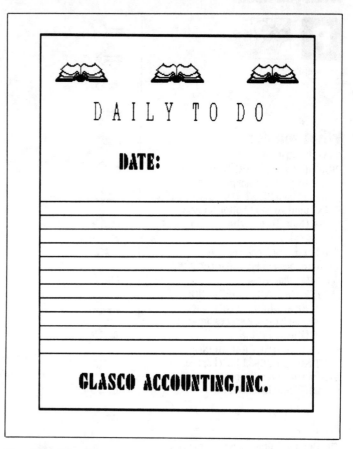

Design Notes:

Lists are easy to produce with the NOTE LINES graphic
printed in a tiled format. For lists of different lengths, just
turn off printer as soon as the number of lines needed have
printed. Your graphic can be personalized to your image, but it
is best to choose either a logo-like graphic or a whimsical,
simple and bold one.

Alternate Graphics
for **BOOK** use **#18** or **#37** or **DOLLAR** (MOD. ART, page 207)

List 2/ WEEKLY TO DO

What you need:

What you do:

SIGN; DYO; BORDER:THICK;
GRAPHIC:BY#(18); SIZE:SM;
LAYOUT:CUSTOM(1); FONT:STENCIL;
MESSAGE:L1(R,■,CH SIZE:L)text,
L3(R,■)text; CENTER:N; Mark your
original print starting point and then
PRINT

*To add CAR graphic, roll back paper to
original print starting point.*

SIGN; DYO; BORDER:NO;
GRAPHIC:OTHER(MOD:CAR, page 178);
SIZE:SM; LAYOUT:CUSTOM(11,13);
FONT:NO; PRINT

*To add REMEMBER graphic, roll back
paper to original print starting point.*

SIGN; DYO; BORDER:NO;
GRAPHIC:OTHER(GL3:REMEMBER –
IBM/GL2); SIZE:SM;
LAYOUT:CUSTOM(12); FONT:NO; PRINT

*To add NOTE LINES, roll back paper to
approximately 2¾ inches below original
print starting point.*

SIGN: DYO; BORDER:NO;
GRAPHIC:OTHER(ORIG:NOTE LINES,
page 169); SIZE:SM; LAYOUT:TILED;
FONT:NO; PRINT (Note: Turn off printer
after the fifteenth line prints or when you
see the NOTE LINES close to the bottom
graphics and then press ESC (←/Comm.)
to exit print mode)

Hints:

Print NOTE LINES last so that you can
see when to turn off the printer.

Design Notes:

This design is generic and can be used with almost any
combination of graphics. The NOTE LINES pattern is simple to
create and can be used in many kinds of designs.

Alternate Graphics
For #18 use #37
For **CAR** use #28
For **REMEMBER** use #18
For **THICK** border use **THIN** border

Mailing Label

What you need:

What you do: ✂ 📖

For top card:
LETTER TOP; DYO;
GRAPHIC:OTHER(MOD:PLANE, page
199); POSITION:LEFT; FONT:STENCIL;
NAME:(L)text; ADDRESS:NO; LINE:N

*Select NO for all LETTERHEAD BOTTOM
choices. Mark your original print
starting point and then PRINT.*

*To add PLANE graphic and second line
of text, roll back paper to approximately
½ inch below original print starting
point.*

LETTER TOP; DYO;
GRAPHIC:OTHER(MOD:PLANE, page
199); POSITION:LEFT;
TEXT:TYPEWRITER; NAME:(L)text;
ADDRESS:NO; LINE:N

*Select NO for all LETTERHEAD BOTTOM
choices and then PRINT.*

*To add PLANE graphic and address, roll
back paper to approximately 3⅞ inches
below original print starting point.*

LETTER TOP; DYO;
GRAPHIC:OTHER(MOD:PLANE, page
199); POSITION:LEFT; FONT:NO;
ADDRESS:L1-L3(L)text; LINE:N

*Select NO for all LETTERHEAD BOTTOM
choices and then PRINT.*

For bottom card:
Make identical graphic and text choices
as shown above. For printings, roll back
paper to each of the following points:

Top line: 5½ inches below original
starting point
Second line: 6 inches below original print
starting point
Address: 9⅜ inches below original print
starting point

*Fold paper in half and then cut with
scissors.*

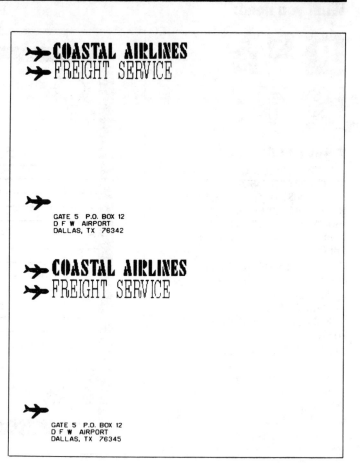

Design Notes:

Mailing labels can be printed out two to a page by rolling
paper forward 5½ inches for second card. Cut labels and
attach to oversized envelope or box with tape. Be sure your
graphics and text do not interfere with the stamp area. Select
a graphic appropriate for your business. For a taller graphic
add about ¼ inch to amount of space between the first and
second lines. (Roll back paper to ¾ inch below original print
starting point.)

Alternate Graphics
For **PLANE** use **JET** (GL2) or **PLANE** (GL1)

Masthead/NEWSLETTER

What you need:

What you do:

SIGN; DYO; BORDER:THIN;
GRAPHIC:OTHER(ORIG:BOAT, page
157); SIZE:SM; LAYOUT:CUSTOM(1,3);
FONT:NEWS; MESSAGE:L1(C,■)text;
CENTER:N; Mark your original print
starting point and then PRINT

*To add additional text, roll back paper
to original print starting point.*

SIGN; DYO; BORDER:NO;
FONT:STENCIL; MESSAGE:(1 space
between all letters):L3(C,■)text;
CENTER:N; PRINT

*To add top rule, roll back paper to
approximately 2⅞ inches below original
print starting point.*

LETTER TOP; DYO; GRAPHIC:NO;
FONT:NO; ADDRESS:NO; LINE:Y

*Select NO for all LETTERHEAD BOTTOM
choices and then PRINT.*

*To add NEWS graphic, roll back paper to
approximately 2¾ inches below original
print starting point.*

LETTER TOP; DYO;
GRAPHIC:OTHER(GL2:NEWS–
IBM/GL1); POSITION:SIX; FONT:NO;
ADDRESS:NO; LINE:Y

*Select NO for all LETTERHEAD BOTTOM
choices and then PRINT.*

*Cover part of NEWS graphic that
extends beyond the border with artist's
white tape or white out liquid.*

Hints:

Prior to reproduction, use artist's white
tape or white out liquid to cover the part
of the NEWS graphic that extends beyond
the border. Your covered up portion won't
be noticed in your copies.

Design Notes:

The Print Shop is an excellent tool for creating school, club or
professional newsletter mastheads. This design incorporates a
simple border to hold the design together and a bold, large
graphic that contrasts with a smaller one.

Meeting Ideas/BRAINSTORMING

What you need:

What you do:

SIGN; DYO; BORDER:NO;
GRAPHIC:OTHER(ORIG:NOTE LINES,
page 169); SIZE:MED:
LAYOUT:STAGGERED; FONT:STENCIL;
MESSAGE:L4(L,■)(type "1," leave 20
spaces and then type "2"),
L9(L,■)(indent 10 spaces and then type
"3"), L14(L,■)(type "4," leave 20 spaces
and then type "5"); CENTER:N; Mark your
original print starting point and then
PRINT

*To add light bulb graphic, roll back
paper to original print starting point.*
SIGN; DYO; BORDER:NO;
GRAPHIC:BY#(18); SIZE:MED;
LAYOUT:STAGGERED; FONT:NO; PRINT

Hints:

Print again and use numbers 6 through 10
for more inspirational cards.

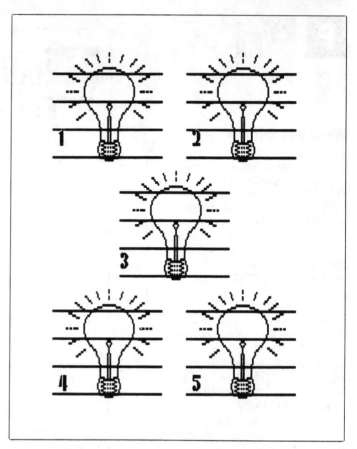

Design Notes:

Sometimes what a brainstorming session most needs is
inspiration. Print and make cards with handwritten or typed
thoughts on back. See suggestions below. You may want to
eliminate the light bulbs and use entire sheet for participants
to jot down their 5 strongest ideas.

Brainstorm Card Ideas:
1. Are you making the big issues little and the little issues big?
Rank the issues.
2. Look at your problem and "think something different."
3. How would a 5-year-old look at this?
4. Stop! Discuss the solutions not the problems.
5. Can you state the problem in one paragraph?

Menu

What you need:

What you do:

For Menu front:
SIGN; DYO; BORDER:NO;
GRAPHIC:OTHER(ORIG:KNIFE & FORK
page 168); SIZE:SM; LAYOUT:CUSTOM(3);
FONT:STENCIL; MESSAGE:L5,L6(R,■)
text; Mark your usual print starting point
and then roll paper forward to approximately 1 inch below this point and PRINT

To add text at bottom, roll back paper to usual print starting point.
SIGN; DYO; BORDER:NO; GRAPHIC:NO;
FONT:PARTY(IBM/STARLET);
MESSAGE:L9,L10(R,■)text; CENTER:N;
PRINT

For Menu inside:
SIGN; DYO; BORDER:NO; GRAPHIC:NO;
FONT:STENCIL; MESSAGE:L1-L2,L4-
L6,L8-L10,L12-L14(R,■)text; CENTER:N;
PRINT (Note: Print on separate sheet or
on back of original sheet. For more about
this, see Hints and Design Notes.)

DAILY
SPECIALS

BILLY'S
DELI

TODAY'S
SPECIALS

ROAST BEEF
ON RYE
ONLY $2.00

PASTRAMI
WITH SWISS
ONLY $2.25

YOGURT
ANY FLAVOR
$ .50 SCOOP

Hints:

Print two sheets of paper as your final art
to be reproduced at a local printer or
copied on a copier. To combine on a
copying machine, copy your menu front
and then refeed your copied sheets back
through the copier to add your menu
inside. Just make sure your sheets are
turned correctly so that your menu inside
is copied in the upright position.

Design Notes:

Print your menu front and menu inside on separate sheets and
then combine in reproduction at a local print shop or on a
copying machine as described in Hints. Or print menu front,
turn over paper and refeed through printer to print menu
inside on back of original sheet. Fold vertically for a new
format! The vertical fold concept works well for cards, menus,
or brochures. For multiple original copies, print about 5 fronts,
turn over and refeed your sheets printing all the menu insides
at one time.

Alternate Graphics
For **KNIFE & FORK** use **#15** or **PLATE** (GL1)

Notepaper

What you need:

What you do: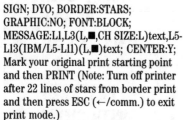

SIGN; DYO; BORDER:STARS;
GRAPHIC:NO; FONT:BLOCK;
MESSAGE:L1,L3(L,■,CH SIZE:L)text,L5-
L13(IBM/L5-L11)(L,■)text; CENTER:Y;
Mark your original print starting point
and then PRINT (Note: Turn off printer
after 22 lines of stars from border print
and then press ESC (←/comm.) to exit
print mode.)

*To add CITY graphic, roll back paper to
approximately 8¾ inches below your
original print starting point.*

SIGN; DYO; BORDER:NO;
GRAPHIC:OTHER(GL2:CITY); SIZE:SM;
LAYOUT:TILED; FONT:NO; PRINT (Note:
Turn off printer as soon as first row prints
and then press ESC (←/comm.) to exit
print mode.)

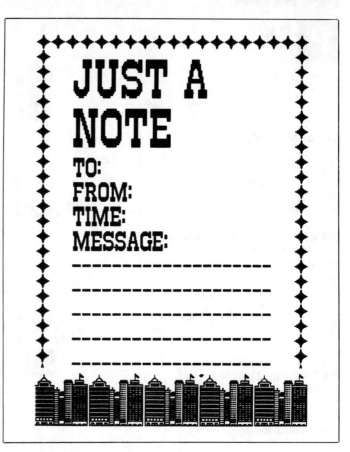

Design Notes:

This design can be used with any Print Shop border and any
graphic appropriate for your purpose. Just remember not to
choose a bold border with a delicate graphic. As shown here,
with planning, notepaper lines can be created quickly and
easily using the "dash" key of the keyboard.

Alternate Graphics
For **CITY** use **FLOWERS** (GL1) or **PARK** (GL1) or **TREE**
(MOD. ART, page 202) or **MR SUN** (GL3–IBM/GL2) or
KEYBOARD (GL2)

Sign 1/CHECKOUT

What you need:

What you do:

SIGN; DYO; BORDER:NO;
GRAPHIC:OTHER(MOD:DOLLAR,
page 207);
LAYOUT:CUSTOM(1,2,3,6,7,8,11,12,13);
FONT:BLOCK(IBM/STENCIL);
MESSAGE:L4,L10(C,■,CH SIZE:L)text;
CENTER:Y; PRINT

Design Notes:

A simple repeat pattern design using a bold graphic is
effective for a sign. For a different look, try a large font
such as NEWS in outline, and then fill in with yellow (or
any brightly colored) marker for a commanding message.

Alternate Graphics
For **DOLLAR** use **#32** or **DOLLAR** (GL2 – IBM/GL1)

Sign 2/DIRECTIONS

What you need:

What you do:

SIGN; DYO; BORDER:THICK;
GRAPHIC:OTHER(ORIG:ARROW 1, page
151); SIZE:LG; FONT:TYPEWRITER;
MESSAGE:L1-L3(2 spaces between all
letters)(C,■)text; Ll4 (2 spaces between
all letters, 4 spaces between words)(C,■)
text; CENTER:N; PRINT

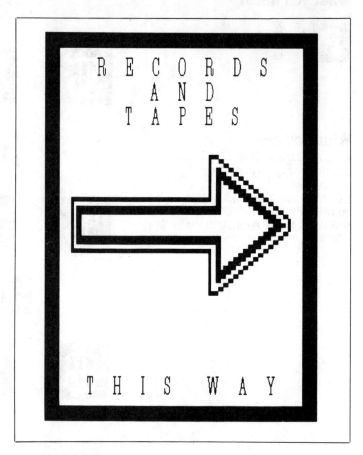

Design Notes:

A simple but bold directional sign is useful for retail
establishments as well as offices for meetings or seminars. *The
Print Shop* is particularly helpful for signs that need to be
created quickly. For a more permanent sign, try photostating
this design to a 150% or 200% enlargement.

Alternate Graphics
For right: **RIGHT** (GL2–IBM/#78) or **ARROW 2** (ORIG. ART,
page 152)
For left: **LEFT** (GL2–IBM/79) or **ARROW** (MOD. ART, page
203)
For up: **UP** (GL2) or **THUMBS UP** (GL3–IBM/#74)
For down: **THUMBS DOWN** (GL3–IBM/#75)

Sign 3/ HELP WANTED

What you need:

What you do:

SIGN; DYO; BORDER:WICKER;
GRAPHIC:NO; FONT:ALEXIA;
MESSAGE:L1,L2(C,■)text; CENTER:N;
Mark your original print starting point
and then PRINT

*To add text in middle, roll back paper to
original print starting point.*

SIGN; DYO; BORDER:NO; GRAPHIC:NO;
FONT:NEWS; MESSAGE:L4,L6(C,■,CH
SIZE:L)text; CENTER:Y; PRINT

*To add additional text in middle, roll
back paper to original print starting
point.*

SIGN; DYO; BORDER:NO; GRAPHIC:NO;
FONT:BLOCK(IBM/REPORTER);
MESSAGE:L11,L12(C,■)text; CENTER:N;
PRINT

*To add text at bottom, roll back paper to
approximately 1 inch above original
print starting point.*

LETTER TOP; DYO; GRAPHIC:NO;
FONT:NO; ADDRESS:NO; LINE:N

LETTER BOTTOM; GRAPHIC:NO;
FONT:NO; ADDRESS:L1-L3(C)text;
LINE:N; PRINT

Design Notes:

Contrast is the single most important quality of a good design.
Varying the sizes of the same font and using different fonts
creates interesting designs without the use of a single graphic.
Using the letterhead mode, a longer message can be added in
a small size that won't interfere with your design.

Sign 4/HOURS 1

What you need:

What you do:

SIGN; DYO; BORDER:NO; GRAPHIC:NO;
FONT:PARTY; MESSAGE:L1,L3(C,■,CH
SIZE:L)text; CENTER:N; Mark your
original print starting point and then
PRINT (IBM/mark your usual print
starting point, move paper to
approximately ½ inch above this point
and then PRINT)

*To add text at bottom, roll back paper
to original print starting point
(IBM/usual print starting point).*

SIGN; DYO; BORDER:NO; GRAPHIC:NO;
FONT:STENCIL; MESSAGE:L10,L12-
L14(C,■)text; CENTER:N; PRINT

*To add flower graphic, roll back paper to
approximately 4½ inches below original
print starting point.*

SIGN; DYO; BORDER:NO;
GRAPHIC:BY#(11); SIZES:M;
LAYOUT:TILED; FONT:NO; PRINT
(Note: Turn off printer after first
row of graphic prints and then press ESC
(←/Comm.) to exit print mode.)

Hints:

Apply double-sided tape to front of sign to
attach to store window.

FLOWERS
BY LISA

HOURS:

9 TO 5 M-F
9 TO 1 SAT.
CLOSED SUN.

Design Notes:

Two signs stacked one on top of the other can make a very
effective large sign. This sign can be stacked on top of Sign 5,
shown on the next page. This particular configuration allows
for flexibility – the bottom sign can be added and removed as
needed. Select a graphic appropriate to your business.

Alternate Graphics
For #11 use **FLOWER** (GL1) or **ART** (GL1) or **CAMERA**
(GL2 – IBM/GL1) or **INSTRUMENTS** (GL2)

Sign 5/ HOURS 2

What you need:

What you do:

SIGN; DYO; BORDER:NO; GRAPHIC:NO;
FONT:NEWS;
MESSAGE:L3,L5,L7(C,■)text; CENTER:Y;
Mark your original print starting point
and then PRINT

*To add flower graphic at top and bottom,
roll back paper to original print
starting point.*

LETTER TOP; DYO; GRAPHIC:BY#(11);
POSITION:SIX; FONT:NO; ADDRESS:NO;
LINE:N

LETTER BOTTOM: GRAPHIC:BY#(11);
POSITION:SIX; FONT:NO; ADDRESS:NO;
LINE:N; PRINT

Hints:

To attach to store window, apply double-
sided tape to front of sign.

Design Notes:

This sign can be stacked below Sign 4, shown on the previous
page. Add and remove this sign as needed. Select a graphic
best suited to your business or message.

Sign 6/SHELF

What you need:

What you do: ✂

SIGN; DYO; BORDER:NO;
GRAPHIC:OTHER(ORIG:BOOK, page
158); SIZE:MED; LAYOUT:CUSTOM(1,4);
FONT:PARTY(IBM/STARLET);
MESSAGE:L1,L2,L8,L9(R,■)text;
CENTER:N; PRINT

Hints:

Select an appropriate graphic, then
consult your template as well as the
Graphics Specifications and The Fonts
sections to be sure your words can clear
your graphic. For easier planning, select
one of the smaller (narrower and
shorter) graphics such as the BOOK.

Design Notes:

Use a bold and descriptive graphic to communicate your
message. Shelf signs need to be easy to read from a distance as
well as up close. Print two shelf signs to a page, then fold in
half and cut.

Alternate Graphics
For **BOOK** use **#23** or **#28** or **#29** or **RIGHT** (GL3 –
IBM/#78) or **LEFT** (GL3 – IBM/#79) or **THUMBS UP** (GL3 –
IBM/#74) or **THUMBS DOWN** (GL3 – IBM/#75) or **SHIP**
(GL2) or **BAND** (GL2)

Sign 7/PROMOTION

What you need:

P **1** **2**

(App/ Comm only)

What you do:

SIGN; DYO; BORDER:THIN; GRAPHIC:OTHER(GL1:MOON); SIZE:MED; LAYOUT:CUSTOM(5); FONT:STENCIL; MESSAGE:L1(1 space between all letters)(C,■)text,L3,L5(C,3D,CH SIZE:L)text; CENTER:N; Mark your original print starting point and then PRINT

To add MOVIE graphic, roll back paper to original print starting point.

SIGN; DYO; BORDER:NO; GRAPHIC:OTHER(GL2:MOVIE – IBM/GL1); SIZE:MED; LAYOUT:CUSTOM(4); FONT:NO; PRINT

To add small text, roll back paper to approximately 4⅝ inches below original print starting point.

LETTER TOP; DYO; GRAPHIC:NO; FONT:NO; ADDRESS:L1(1 space between all letters, 2 spaces between words)(C)text,L2,L3(C)text; LINE:N

Select NO for all LETTERHEAD BOTTOM choices and then PRINT.

Hints:

Create a "picture" by choosing two graphics that relate to one another.

Design Notes:

By using the sign mode for the headline and graphics of a sign, flyer or ad, you can then add more detailed text in a small size with the letterhead mode. The graphics you choose depend on your message, but below are some suggested pairs.

Alternate Graphics

Use **#19** at left, **#20** at right

Use **PLATE** (GL1) at left, **#15** or **COFFEE** (GL3 – IBM/GL2) at right

Use **RIGHT** (GL3 – IBM/#78) at left, **PHONE** (GL1) at right

Sign 8/ DAILY SPECIALS (STACKED)

What you need:

What you do:

To create TOP sign:
LETTER TOP; DYO; GRAPHIC:BY#(14);
POSITION:SIX; FONT:NO; ADDRESS:NO;
LINE:N

Select NO for all LETTERHEAD BOTTOM choices. Mark your original print starting point and then PRINT.

To add second row of cones, roll paper back to approximately 1¼ inches below original print starting point.

SIGN; DYO; BORDER:NO;
GRAPHIC:BY#(14); SIZE:SM;
LAYOUT:CUSTOM(1,2,3); FONT:NO;
PRINT

To add third row of cones, roll back paper to approximately 3½ inches below original print starting point.

SIGN; DYO; BORDER:NO;
GRAPHIC:BY#(14); SIZE:MED;
LAYOUT:CUSTOM(1,2); FONT:NO; PRINT

To add message at bottom, roll back paper to approximately ⅞ inch below original print starting point.

SIGN; DYO; BORDER:NO; GRAPHIC:NO;
FONT:PARTY(IBM/STARLET);
MESSAGE:L7,L9(C,■,CH SIZE:L)text;
CENTER:N; PRINT

To create BOTTOM sign:
SIGN; DYO; BORDER:NO;
GRAPHIC:NO; FONT:PARTY;
MESSAGE(1 space between all
letters):L1,L3,L5,L7(C,□)text; CENTER:Y;
Mark your original print starting point
and then PRINT

To add cones at bottom, roll back paper to original print starting point.

LETTER TOP; DYO; GRAPHIC:NO;
FONT:NO; ADDRESS:NO; LINE:N

LETTER BOTTOM; GRAPHIC:BY#(14);
POSITION:SIX; FONT:NO; ADDRESS:NO;
LINE:N; PRINT

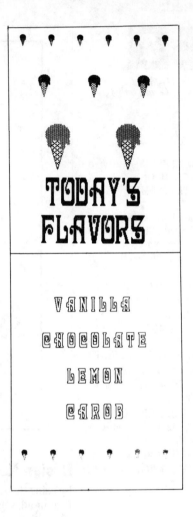

Stack signs and attach with tape on back. Top sign should overlap bottom sign about 1 inch.

Design Notes:

Large signs can be created from several 8½ x 11 sheets. Here a vertical format is shown. A 17 x 22 sign can be created with four sheets. A single design repeated can also be very effective. Try a row of six or block of four on a wall, in a window or on a bulletin board.

New And Modified Art

- WHAT'S IN THIS SECTION

- USING THIS SECTION

- THE NEW ART PAGE

- THE MODIFIED PRINT SHOP ART PAGE

- ART OVERVIEW

 NEW ART

 MODIFIED ART

What's in This Section

This is a section of alternatives—art alternatives. There is new art you can easily copy, alternative looks for the existing Print Shop graphics, and techniques you can use to create an alternative graphic library of your very own. It's the section to turn to when you're thinking about a Print Shop design and need to find a new art idea—or need to freshen up an old one.

Highlighted for you here (and first introduced on page 4) is an overview of what you'll find in this section.

New Art: You'll find easy-to-create original art—more pictures, more symbols.

Modified Print Shop Art: You'll find many Print Shop favorites—with an entirely new look or even transformed into a completely different object.

Art Techniques: You'll find easy-to-copy techniques you can use when you want to give your own graphic choices a new look or identity.

Design Ideas: You'll find suggestions and applications (more design ideas!) to give you a sense of the look or feel each graphic can contribute to a design.

Art Overview: You'll find reduced samples of every piece of handbook art all in one place—on the art overview page.

Using This Section

The art overview page is an excellent place to start! At a glance you'll see every piece of new and modified art – you'll know exactly what lies ahead. Well, almost. As in Designs, Designs, Designs, the printed samples are a key element of the section. Yet, they represent only a portion of what's included.

To get the most out of New and Modified Art, look beyond the printed samples. Throughout the section are many design ideas not found elsewhere in the handbook. And many techniques for inputting and modifying art are sure to come in handy for your own work.

Highlighted for you here (and explained on pages 7-8) are suggestions for using this section.

SUGGESTION #1: Always keep the art overview page in mind. It's a great place to start thinking about a look for your design.

SUGGESTION #2: Copy, adapt, embellish! When you find a piece of art you like, by all means copy it. If the art is not exactly right for your design, add your own personal touch and adapt it for your own special purpose.

SUGGESTION #3: Modify any Print Shop graphic. The handbook's techniques for modifying art are easy to copy and can be applied to any Print Shop graphic. In many cases, a particular graphic was selected simply to illustrate an art modification technique.

SUGGESTION #4: The New and Modified Art pages show how a piece of art can be used to create a certain look or convey a special message. Use the design ideas – copy them or adapt them.

SUGGESTION #5: If a modified art example uses a Print Shop package you don't have, don't flip past it. On the page are likely to be ideas and techniques you can easily apply to other graphics. And if you're really in love with the graphic, simply treat it as new art – copy the graphic, input it from scratch!

SUGGESTION #6: Let the handbook's art be a springboard for new art ideas of your own.

Symbols: A Review

Every art sample is clearly marked with the following easy-to-recognize symbols to let you know immediately if more than *The Print Shop* program was used to create it. (If you're in the Modified Art section and see a graphic you really like but don't have the appropriate Print Shop package, remember: you can treat the graphic as new art and copy it from scratch!)

P The Print Shop

1 Graphics Library 1

2 Graphics Library 2

3 Graphics Library 3

H Holiday Edition

About the Art Grid

(REMINDER: The IBM symbols appear next to the Apple and Commodore symbols only when they differ from the Apple and Commodore versions.)

Every new and modified art sample is positioned on an art grid. The grid looks just like graph paper, composed of many small boxes. The grid is used to represent *The Print Shop* Graphic Editor drawing area. Each small box represents a dot that can be filled in with the Graphic Editor. The handbook grid shows the position of every possible dot on the Graphic Editor drawing surface. Every tenth box on the grid is labeled and highlighted to make it easy for you to identify the position of a box.

In the Graphic Editor, the position of every dot is identified on screen by an x – coordinate and a y – coordinate. The position of the dot from left to right is called the x – coordinate. The position of the dot from top to bottom is called the y – coordinate. For example, if you want to fill in a dot that is 25 dots across and 30 dots down, just move your cursor on the Graphic Editor drawing surface to the position labeled $x = 25, y = 30$ and you're all set.

The numbers on the art grid correspond to the numbers on screen. A box on the art grid that is 25 boxes across and 30 boxes down corresponds to the dot on screen that is 25 dots across and 30 dots down. The box corresponds to the dot labeled $x = 25, y = 30$.

Inputting the Handbook Art

Fill in the dots on screen in the same positions as shown in the art grid. To input art from the New Art section, go to the Graphic Editor and fill in the dots on screen from scratch. To input art from the Modified Art section, go to the Graphic Editor, and call up the graphic to be modified. Keep or add all the dots shown in black on the art grid. Erase the dots shown in light grey. You'll have a new piece of art at your disposal–save it to use again and again. *(Note:* Try to copy the same pattern of dots on screen as shown in the art grid. But don't be concerned if you don't copy every single dot. Even if 90% of the dots match up, your art is likely to look just like the handbook's!)

If you don't have the appropriate Print Shop package for a modified art sample, don't rush past that page. You can treat the sample as new art and input it from scratch. Just fill in the dots on screen in the same positions as the black boxes on the grid. (Ignore the light grey boxes–they represent the positions of dots to be erased when modifying!)

Inputting Your Own Original Art

Many Print Shop users take advantage of the Graphic Editor to create original graphics. With the blank art grid on page 291 of the Planning Tools section, you can sketch your creation in pencil ahead of time (just copy the grid on a copying machine), fine tune your artwork, and then head for your computer. Use your art grid drawing as a guide to filling in the appropriate dots on the Graphic Editor drawing surface.

The New Art Page

The reduced page shown here provides an explanation of the various elements you'll find with every piece of new art.

Faces: Art Sample Name—identifies the specific item shown.

What You Need: The Print Shop symbol always appears here—you'll never need more in the New Art section!

Category Symbol: Symbol on top right tells you if you're in the New Art or Modified Art section.

Ideas: A variety of information including alternative suggestions for modifying and using the art may appear here.

Applications: Samples in Designs, Designs, Designs that use the art are listed by page number. Additional designs using the art are also shown here.

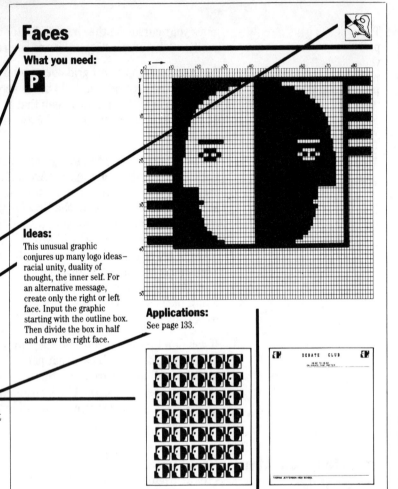

Faces

What you need:

P

Ideas:
This unusual graphic conjures up many logo ideas—racial unity, duality of thought, the inner self. For an alternative message, create only the right or left face. Input the graphic starting with the outline box. Then divide the box in half and draw the right face.

Applications:
See page 133.

The Art: An actual print out of the art is shown in position on the art grid. Just call up the Graphic Editor on your Print Shop disk. Fill in the dots on the Graphic Editor drawing surface in the same positions as shown on the art grid, save your work, and you'll have a new piece of art at your disposal. (*Note:* Try to copy the same pattern of dots on screen as shown in the art grid. But don't be concerned if you don't copy every single dot. Even if 90% of the dots match up, your art is likely to look just like the handbook's!)

The Modified Print Shop Art Page

The reduced page shown here provides an explanation of the various elements you'll find with every piece of modified Print Shop art.

Arrow: Art Sample Name – identifies the specific item shown.

What You Need: Easy-to-recognize symbols (shown on page 10) tell you what Print Shop programs were used to create the art.

Before & After: Shows what the art looks like before and after the changes are made.

Category Symbol: Symbol at top right tells you if you're in the New Art or Modified Art section.

Ideas: A variety of information including alternative suggestions for modifying and using the art may appear here.

Applications: Samples in Designs, Designs, Designs that use the art are listed by page number. Additional designs for using the art are also shown here.

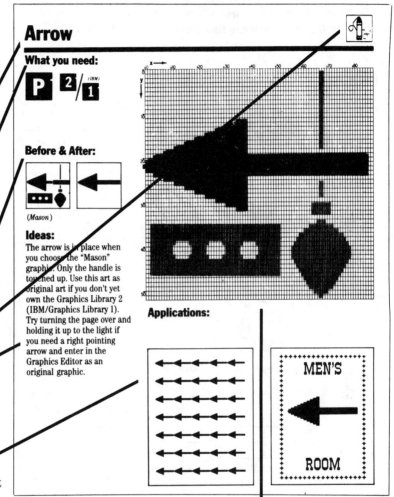

Arrow

What you need:

P **2**/**1** *(IBM)*

Before & After:

(Mason)

Ideas:
The arrow is in place when you choose the "Mason" graphic. Only the handle is touched up. Use this art as original art if you don't yet own the Graphics Library 2 (IBM/Graphics Library 1). Try turning the page over and holding it up to the light if you need a right pointing arrow and enter in the Graphics Editor as an original graphic.

Applications:

MEN'S

ROOM

The Art: An actual printout of the art is shown in position on the art grid. Every tenth box is labeled for easy identification. All boxes to be kept from the original graphic or to be added by you are shown in black. All boxes to be erased by you are shown in light grey. *(Note:* Try to copy the same pattern of dots on the screen as shown in the art grid. But don't be concerned if you don't copy every single dot. Even if 90% of the dots match up, your art is likely to look just like the handbook's!)

Art Overview

All the handbook's new and modified art is shown here. Use these
pages for quick reference to find a graphic with the right look for
your design.

New Art

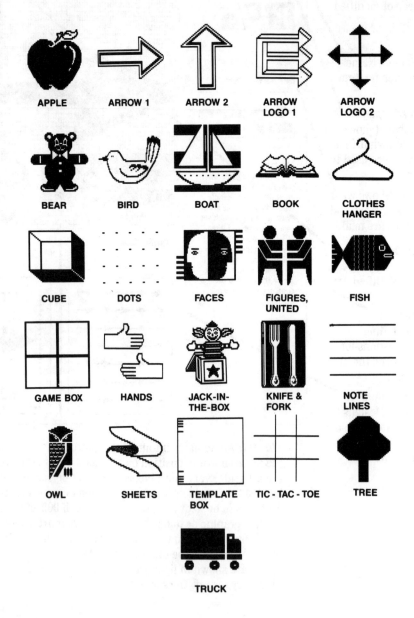

APPLE ARROW 1 ARROW 2 ARROW LOGO 1 ARROW LOGO 2

BEAR BIRD BOAT BOOK CLOTHES HANGER

CUBE DOTS FACES FIGURES, UNITED FISH

GAME BOX HANDS JACK-IN-THE-BOX KNIFE & FORK NOTE LINES

OWL SHEETS TEMPLATE BOX TIC - TAC - TOE TREE

TRUCK

Modified Art

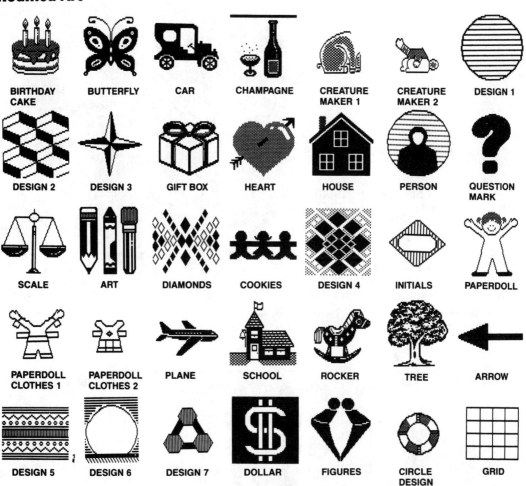

BIRTHDAY CAKE BUTTERFLY CAR CHAMPAGNE CREATURE MAKER 1 CREATURE MAKER 2 DESIGN 1

DESIGN 2 DESIGN 3 GIFT BOX HEART HOUSE PERSON QUESTION MARK

SCALE ART DIAMONDS COOKIES DESIGN 4 INITIALS PAPERDOLL

PAPERDOLL CLOTHES 1 PAPERDOLL CLOTHES 2 PLANE SCHOOL ROCKER TREE ARROW

DESIGN 5 DESIGN 6 DESIGN 7 DOLLAR FIGURES CIRCLE DESIGN GRID

POINTING FINGER SHADOW BOX TRIANGLE

Apple

What you need:

Ideas:

The "Apple" graphic works as both a symbol or logo for a company or organization as well as a great decorative piece of art. It can be used to communicate education, healthful eating or even preventative care. Child care centers, educational consultants, tutors, public television stations, health food stores or even fruit and vegetable vendors can create personalized signs, letterheads or business cards with this graphic.

Applications:

See page 72.

Arrow 1

What you need:

Ideas:

A large graphic arrow makes an excellent communicative symbol. This "Arrow" is designed in outline form for design interest and to allow for highlighting with brightly colored markers. Try using the arrow on a banner in a hallway or a door sign for directions. Printed large and colored in, the arrow will quickly deliver your message. The thickness of the inside black border provides safety for coloring in smaller-sized arrows on a card or wrapping paper design.

To create a right facing arrow, copy this page and hold it up to the light. (Note: Your version of *The Print Shop* program may allow you to print this graphic backward for a reverse arrow.)

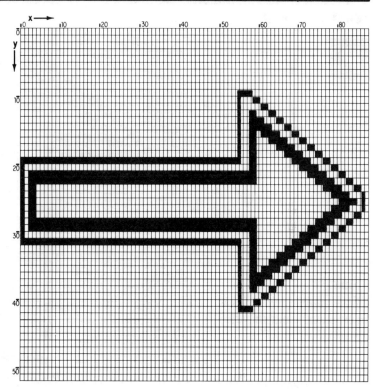

Applications:

See page 125.

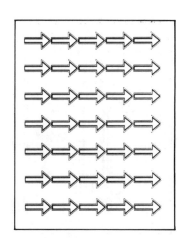

Arrow 2

What you need:

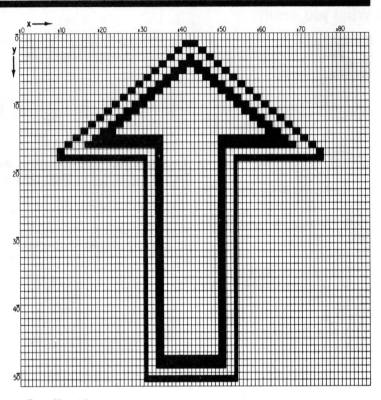

Ideas:

A large graphic arrow makes an excellent communicative symbol. This "Arrow" is designed in outline form for design interest and to allow for highlighting with brightly colored markers. Try using the arrow on a banner in a hallway or a door sign for directions. Printed large and colored in, the arrow will quickly deliver your message. The thickness of the inside black border provides safety for coloring in smaller-sized arrows on a card or wrapping paper design.

To create a downward pointing arrow, copy this page and hold it up to the light.

Applications:

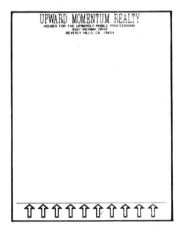

Arrow Logo 1

What you need:

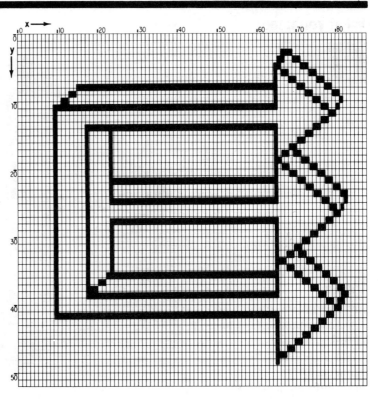

Ideas:

Arrows incorporated into a symbol design make a strong, aggressive statement. To make this graphic bolder, try blackening in the planes that create the 3-D effect. A different look can be created by blackening in only the 3-D planes facing the right side. This art can also be used as the basis of a cube by erasing the arrow heads and closing off the right side.

Applications:

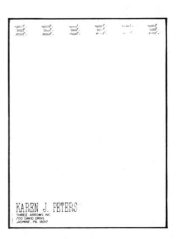

Arrow Logo 2

What you need:

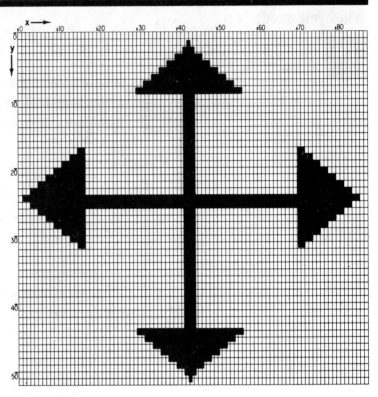

Ideas:

Arrows work so well with *The Print Shop* program because of their simplicity and boldness. A multi-directional arrow symbol can create many different looks depending upon the application. This graphic can also be used as the basis for a diamond outline or crest.

Applications:

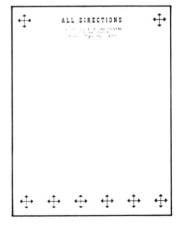

Bear

What you need:

Ideas:

This "Bear" makes a terrific "logo" for a young child, a toy or gift store, or even a school or organization charity project. To input the bear, start with his arms, and then move on to his body.

Applications:

See page 65.

Bird

What you need:

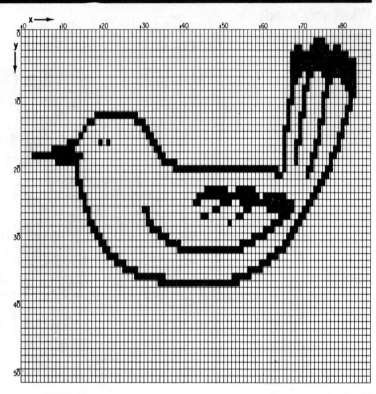

Ideas:

A very simple and bold bird is an appropriate symbol for many applications. Try using this generic graphic with many of the designs shown in Designs, Designs, Designs. Children's wrapping paper, friendship cards, personalized memos, letterheads or business cards are good basic applications for this graphic.

Applications:

See page 41.

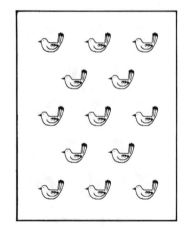

Boat

What you need:

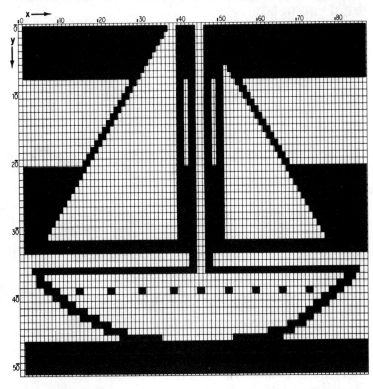

Ideas:

Graphics designed to fill the Graphics Editor box make interesting patterns when printed in duplicate next to one another. This "Boat" graphic looks particularly nautical in its repetition due to the bold stripes. For a simpler graphic create the boat without the background stripes.

Applications:

See page 129.

Book

What you need:

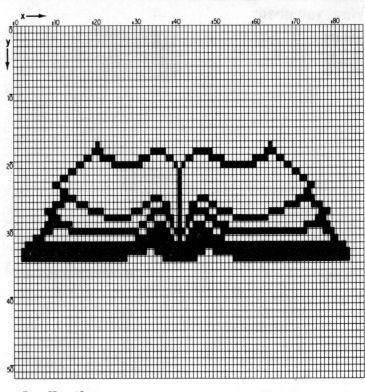

Ideas:

Writers, schools, clubs, bookstores, publishers can all benefit from a simple open book symbol. This graphic works both as a symbol and decorative piece of art. It's also the perfect graphic to use for book gift wrap.

Applications:

See page 126.

Clothes Hanger

What you need:

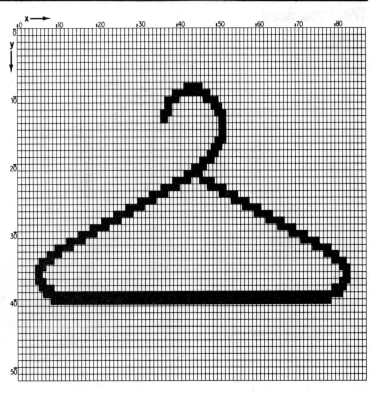

Ideas:

This graphic is easy to create and can be used as a logo for clothing stores, dry cleaners, charity drives, or closet signs. It's also a fun graphic to repeat in the sign mode for gift wrap for any clothing-related gifts such as shirts and ties.

Applications:

See page 122.

Cubes

What you need:

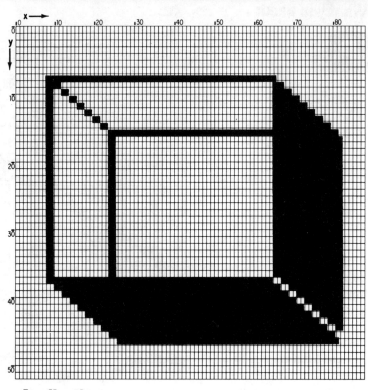

Ideas:

The cube is a strong basic shape for many applications. Try putting your personal, company or organization initials inside for a crest look. Print large- or medium-sized cubes in the sign mode and use the frames for children's drawings. Print multiple copies or copy on a copying machine for car trips!

Applications:

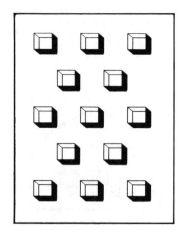

Dots

What you need:

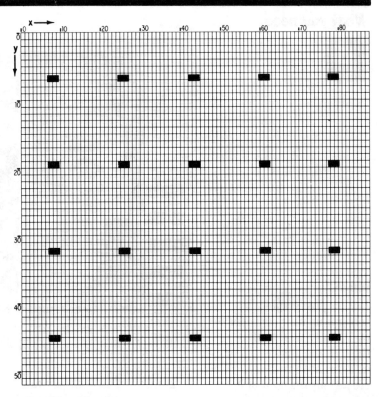

Ideas:

Repeated "Dots" make a
great pattern behind other
Print Shop graphics. Just
print the dots, roll back your
paper to your print starting
point, and then print another
graphic over the dots. This
graphic can also be used to
create the "game board" of a
fun dot-connecting game. For
more about this, see page 85.

Applications:

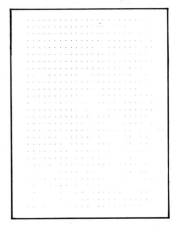

Faces

What you need:

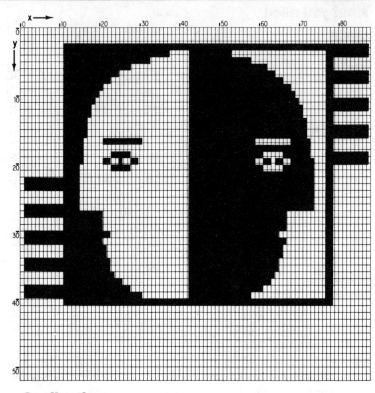

Ideas:

This unusual graphic conjures up many logo ideas– racial unity, duality of thought, the inner self. For an alternative message, create only the right or left face. Input the graphic starting with the outline box. Then divide the box in half and draw the right face.

Applications:

See page 133.

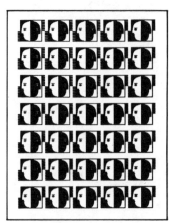

Figures, United

What you need:

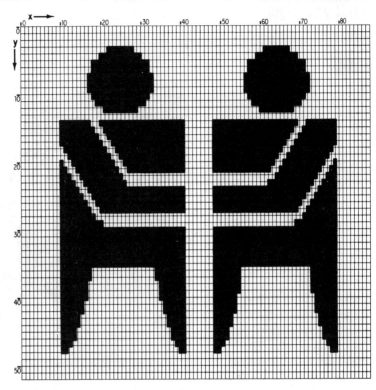

Ideas:

This graphic makes an ideal symbol for a message of unity. Blacken in the arm area and use for any kind of people-related message. Figures without legs create more of a "logo" look. A single figure without arms conveys the notion of "man"; a triangular base can be drawn to convey the notion of "woman".

Applications:

See page 121.

Fish

What you need:

P

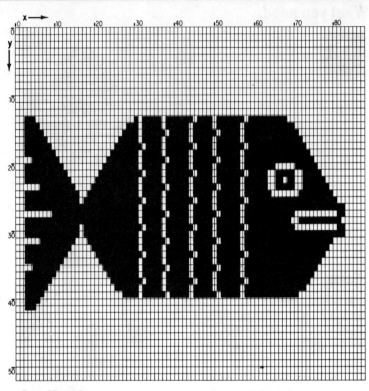

Ideas:

A graphic with a simple shape and some degree of detail is very effective for Print Shop designs. The "Fish" can be used as a fun logo for personal designs or as a professional logo for businesses that deal with seafood, the ocean, fishing, boating, and so on. This graphic also works well in a repeat pattern for signs and wrapping paper.

Applications:

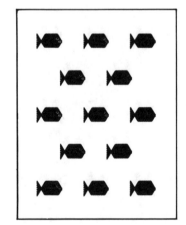

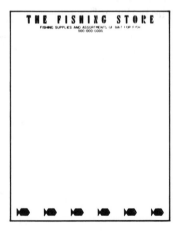

THE FISHING STORE
FISHING SUPPLIES AND ASSORTMENTS OF BAIT FOR FISH
000-000-0000

Game Box

What you need:

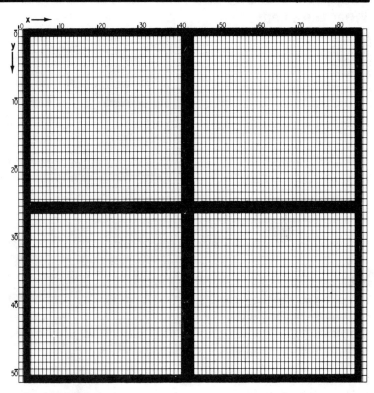

Ideas:

This graphic is used to create the puzzle/game box shown in Designs, Designs, Designs on page 82. Draw the box directly over a Print Shop graphic (animal, car or whatever you choose). Then cut into four pieces to make a child's jigsaw puzzle. The "Game Box" graphic also works well in repetition in a row for a letterhead, as a sign background or wrapping paper design.

Applications:

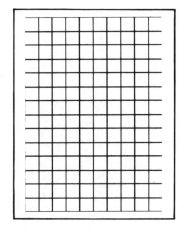

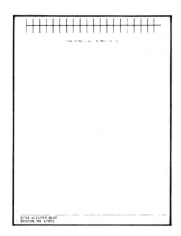

Hands

What you need:

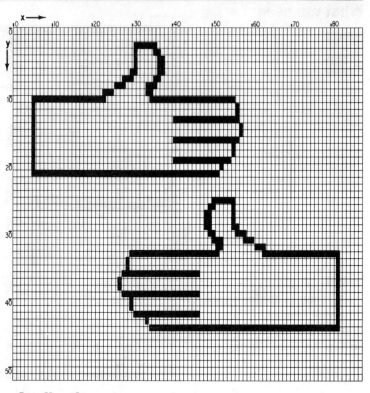

Ideas:

The message of unity and cooperation implied by this graphic makes it applicable to many different situations. Its generic quality of friendship also makes it a good choice for a decorative graphic. For a different look, draw a large outline box around the hands. For another look, fill in the box as shown in the modified "Dollar" sign graphic on page 00.

Applications:

See page 37.

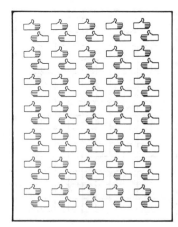

Jack-in-the-Box

What you need:

Ideas:

Toy stores, child care centers, party services are examples of the many possible applications for this "Jack-in-the-Box" graphic. The graphic also makes a perfect personal symbol for a child or the young at heart. In repetition the graphic is effective for wrapping paper or sign backgrounds. The box with the star inside is a useful decorative object by itself!

Applications:

See page 54.

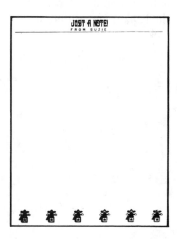

Knife & Fork

What you need:

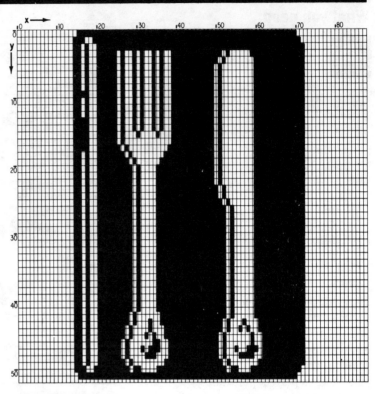

Ideas:

Restaurants, houseware/gift shops, sales representatives of any food service or kitchen goods can benefit from the "Knife & Fork" graphic. A catering or party consultant can use the graphic to design a business card or letterhead. The knife and fork can be outlined and drawn without the napkin for a different look.

Applications:

See page 131.

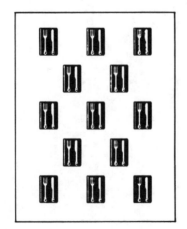

Note Lines

What you need:

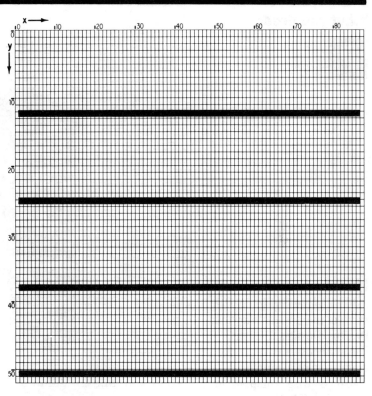

Ideas:

These four lines were carefully positioned for creating ruled note paper. Input the lines exactly as shown, then choose small graphic, tiled in the sign mode. Your lines will be evenly spaced on the page when they print!

Applications:

See page 130.

Owl

What you need:

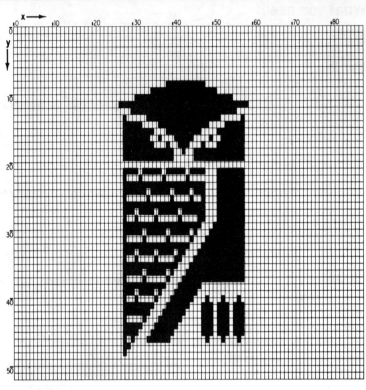

Ideas:

Use this generic graphic with many of the designs shown in Designs, Designs, Designs. Use as an alternative graduation card graphic, a logo for a "wise" company on a letterhead, business card or mailing label, for example.

Applications:

See page 96.

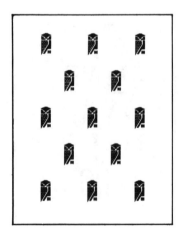

Sheets

What you need:

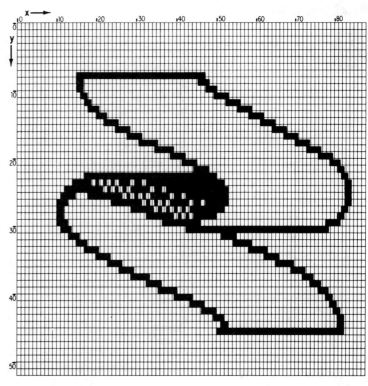

Ideas:

This graphic makes a perfect symbol for fabric, paper or film. Fill in the entire shape to create a new look that implies "fanfare" – perfect for a variety of decorative uses.

Applications:

See page 112.

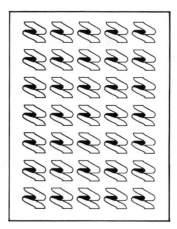

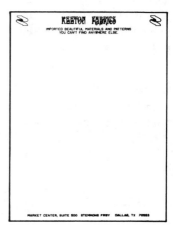

Template Box

What you need:

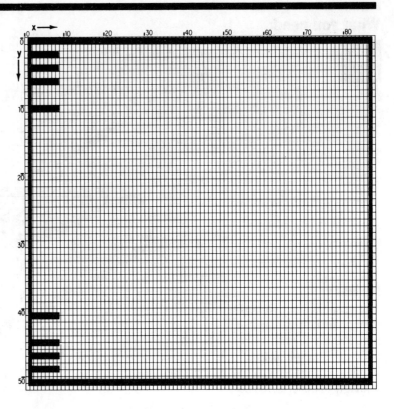

Ideas:

The "Template Box" is to be used in templates that serve as guideline forms for your own original Print Shop creations. Templates using the "Template Box" were produced and used for creating designs in this book. For an explanation of templates, their use and how you can create your own, turn to the Planning Tools section pages 215-252.

Applications:

Here are two sample templates. See more on pages 236-252.

Sign/Card

Font: Alexia/small
Graphic: Small/staggered

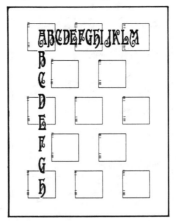

Sign/Card

Font: News/large
Graphic: Medium/staggered

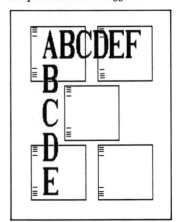

Tic-Tac-Toe

What you need:

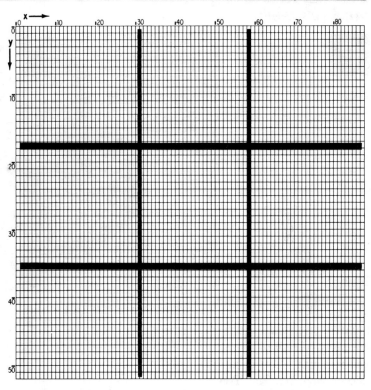

Ideas:

A "Tic-Tac-Toe" graphic is easy to create with the Print Shop's Graphic Editor. Print out lots of sheets in the sign mode. Just choose the medium-size graphic in staggered and you have a great travel or waiting game. The graphic also can be used to create an interesting symbol or repeat decorative pattern. Blacken in the center box to create a graphic with another look.

Applications:

See page 83.

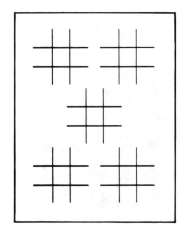

Tree

What you need:

Ideas:

Most Print Shop graphics are illustrative pieces of art. This quality makes them perfect for use as spot art to communicate a story or as decorative pieces. The "Tree" is an example of a different graphic approach. A very simple yet bold shape is used to "suggest" an object, in this case a tree. The graphic is a symbol. To center the tree more easily, draw the tree's trunk first.

Applications:

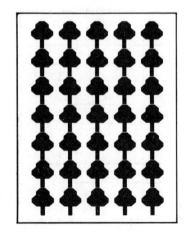

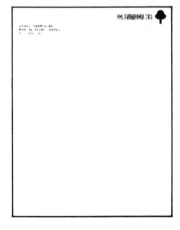

Truck

What you need:

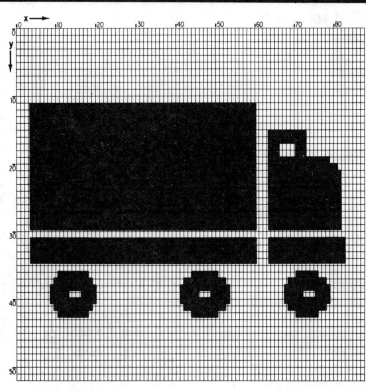

Ideas:

The "Truck" is another example of very simple and bold art that can be created with *The Print Shop's* Graphic Editor. Graphics that have a "symbolic" look as shown here, can be used in broad applications. This truck, for example, works equally well in a sign for a moving company, toy store, or child's room.

Applications:

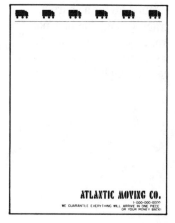

Birthday Cake

What you need:

Before & After:

(#1)

Ideas:

Celebrate with up to five candles – perfect for the birthday of a one to five-year-old. Move the two outside candles in five panels. Then two additional candles can be added on either side. Line these two candles up with the base of the center candle. The cake is strengthened and cleaned up for a sharper graphic look. You may not want to take the time to do more than "personalize" your cake for a child's age.

Applications:

See page 62.

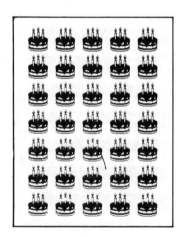

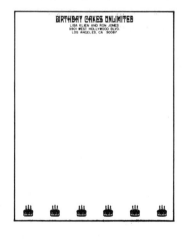

Butterfly

What you need:

Before & After:

(#49)

Ideas:

Many Print Shop graphics can be used for logos when they are merely made more black. The butterfly is a good example of how a decorative piece of art can be turned into a symbol or logo with a little Graphic Editor work. Try different wing patterns or fill in completely!

Applications:

See page 80.

Car

What you need:

Before & After:

(#28)

Ideas:

When the car is silhouetted, it becomes a symbol or logo applicable to many more uses. You may want to use it for a very specific idea as shown here or a more generic use such as a school or club car wash. Try erasing the car above the windows to create a jeep for new uses... camping, rentals, tour rides.

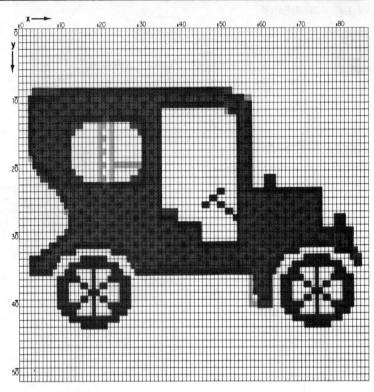

Applications:
See page 84.

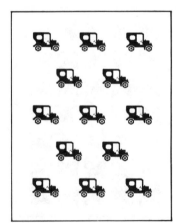

GOOD AS NEW ANTIQUE CARS, INC.

BILL PIERCE AND SONS
4061 HARPER ROAD
EASTVILLE, NEW HAMPSHIRE

Champagne

What you need:

Before & After:

(#16)

Ideas:

Blacken in the champagne bottle for a strong graphic look. Add a hairline above or below the art to create a symbol look. Then when your new art is printed in multiples, either "tiled" or in a row, a new statement is made.

Applications:

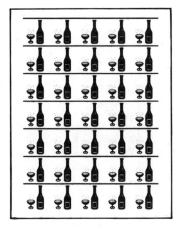

Creature Maker-1

What you need:

Before & After:

(#45)

Ideas:

Kids can play for hours at home, at a restaurant or in the car with headless Print Shop animals! Print out and copy on a copying machine for hours of silly drawing fun. You can erase the pig's head in any manner as long as you allow room for a child to fill in a new creature.

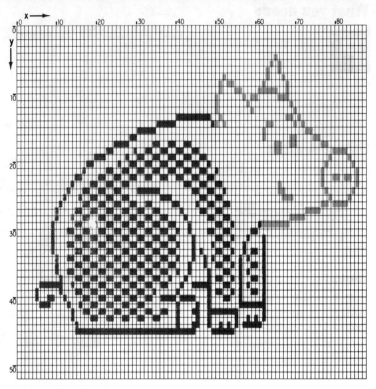

Applications:
See page 79.

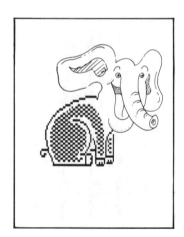 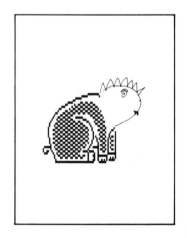

Creature Maker-2

What you need:

Before & After:

(#46)

Ideas:
Many Print Shop graphics
will offer creative play when
modified. Try the penguin,
the cat, the turtle, the bird...
even Santa Claus! Copy a
stack of them for single or
group play.

Applications:

Design 1

What you need:

Before & After:

(#6)

Ideas:

The "Graduate" makes an interesting decorative or symbolic graphic when simplified to its background only. Although it looks better, you may not want to take the time to make the circle thicker as shown here. Use this same Print Shop graphic as a start for circles.

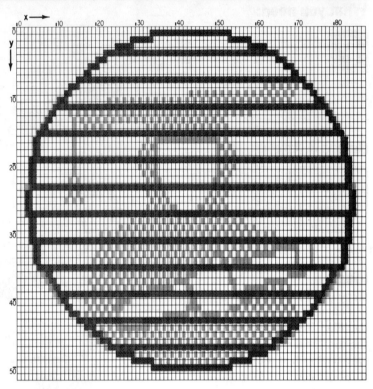

Applications:

Design 2

What you need:

Before & After:

(#54/IBM: #124)

Ideas:

Patterns can be called up in the Graphic Editor and saved on your personal data disk. Alter them as you wish. By erasing the internal scattered dots and blackening in two sides of the design, a 3-D effect is created here. The new graphic is most effective in an overall repeat pattern for a background gift wrap or a repeated row. Try using different colored markers in the white "fences" to create a quilted or Indian look for cards or wrapping paper.

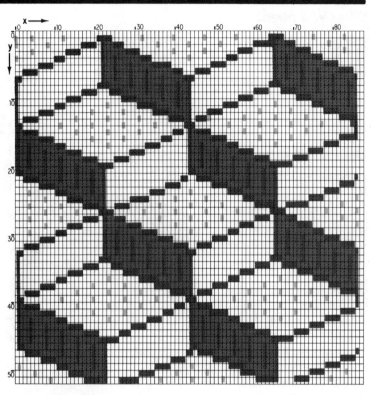

Applications:

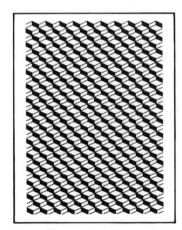 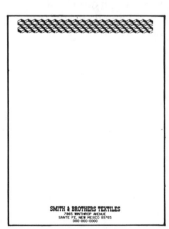

Design 3

What you need:

Before & After:

(#58/IBM: #128)

Ideas:

Patterns can be called up in the Graphic Editor and saved on your personal data disk. A new design can then be created by erasing and adding. Here a "TV screen" star becomes a bold symbol by deleting the background and blackening in the shadowed sides. For an even bolder look, fill in all sides of the star.

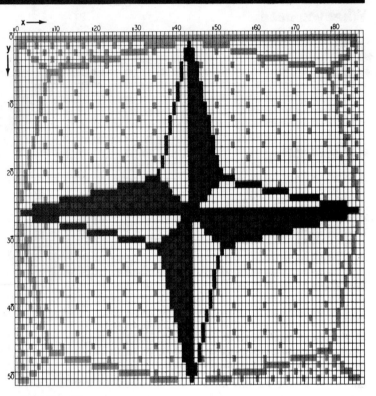

Applications:

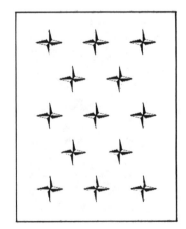 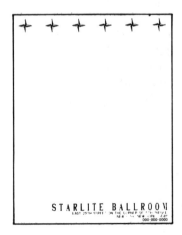

Gift Box

What you need:

Before & After:

(#4)

Ideas:

A little erasing and filling in will enhance this decorative Print Shop graphic for use as a logo or strong background graphic. For gift wrap, try coloring the packages with different colored markers.

Applications:

See page 33.

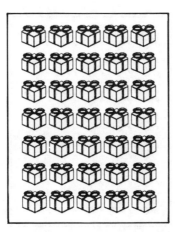

Heart

What you need:

Before & After:

(#3)

Ideas:

The "Heart" can be filled in completely black for a more graphic symbol. The arrow through the heart makes a great graphic for a Valentine's card or banner. Send the banner as a card in a 9″ x 12″ envelope!

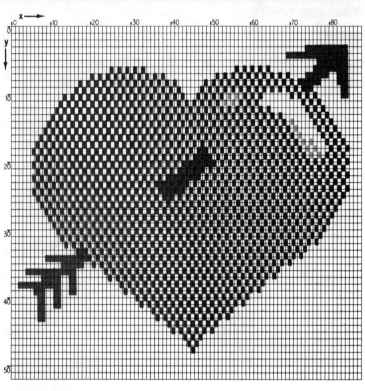

Applications:

See page 42.

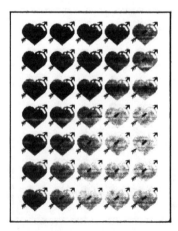

House

What you need:

Before & After:

(#31)

Ideas:

The house can be made even more symbolic by filling in the windows and erasing the chimney. A flattened roof with windows placed on top of one another creates a building symbol.

Applications:

See page 57.

THE BOWMAN'S

3534 INWOOD ROAD
BRYAN, OHIO 43506

Person

What you need:

Before & After:

(#6)

Ideas:

A male or female figure can be created easily for specific applications. A more generic symbol look as shown here works well for "person" communication. Every other line of the background pattern can be filled in on the computer or with various colored markers to add interest. To simplify, erase background totally and square off the base of the figure.

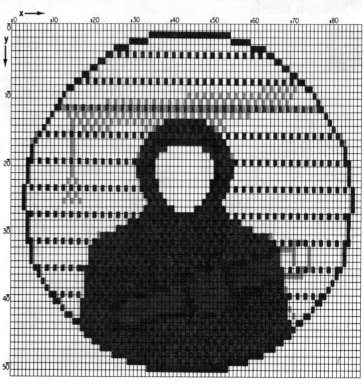

Applications:

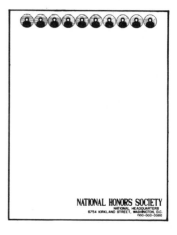

NATIONAL HONORS SOCIETY
NATIONAL HEADQUARTERS
8754 KIRKLAND STREET, WASHINGTON, D.C.
000-000-0000

Question Mark

What you need:

Before & After:

(#38)

Ideas:

Here is the suggested modification to achieve a very graphic symbol. A simpler way of strengthening this Print Shop graphic is to fill in the front plane of the question mark without rounding off the edges or erasing the 3-D side. For a better logo look, erase the 3-D side and blacken in the interior of the remaining art. An exclamation point graphic can also be created. Just fill in the center of the modified question mark and complete the curve.

Applications:

Scale

What you need:

Before & After:

(#35)

Ideas:

The concept of balance or justice can apply to many logo applications. With a little touch-up work in the Graphic Editor, the "Scale" graphic is made bold and clear.

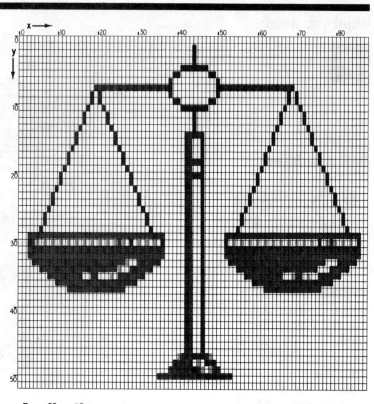

Applications:

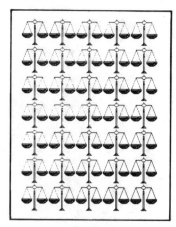

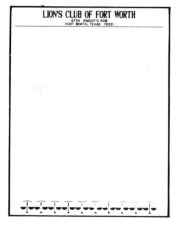

LION'S CLUB OF FORT WORTH
6754 KNIGHT'S ROW
FORT WORTH, TEXAS 76321

Art

What you need:

Before & After:

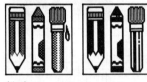

(Art)

Ideas:

Artists, writers, students and a variety of shop owners can use a writing tool or art symbol to represent what they do. The Print Shop graphic is altered slightly here to make a bolder symbol.

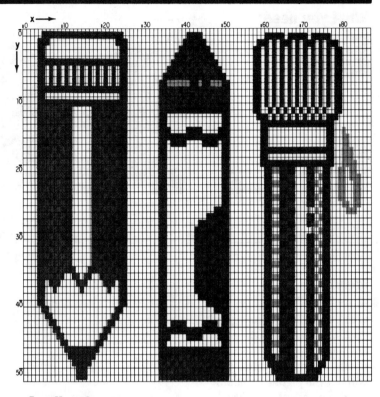

Applications:

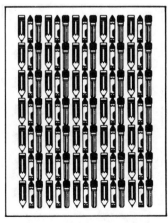

H M S ART SUPPLY
ALL YOU NEED IN ONE PLACE!
546 LOMBARD STREET   SAN FRANCISCO, CA. 78654
000-000-0000

Cookies

What you need:

Before & After:

(*Cookies*)

Ideas:

A "pro-social" symbol is created by silhouetting gingerbread men. The communication of unisex children can be created without the pigtails. A double band can easily be achieved by modifying both the top and bottom gingerbread rows.

Applications:

HAND IN HAND PLAY SCHOOL
1311 SOUTH LOOP 820
FORT WORTH, TEXAS 76132
000-000-0000

Design 4

What you need:

Before & After:

(Snow)

Ideas:

This graphic, which was intended for a tile pattern, works well as a new graphic when modified. It has many possibilities depending on what is erased and what is added in the Graphic Editor. It can remain a good tile pattern or be used as a decorative element.

Applications:

Diamonds

What you need:

Before & After:

(*Diamonds*)

Ideas:

Use this Print Shop graphic to create an interesting new pattern or symbol for letterheads, banners, signs and cards or as an overall pattern. There are several ways you can strengthen this graphic. Each way will create an entirely new look when shown in repetition.

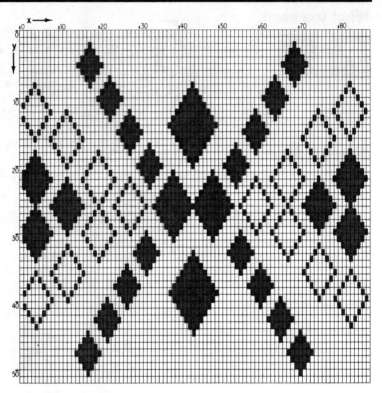

Applications:

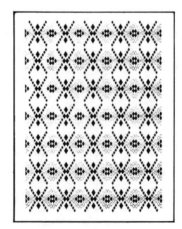

Initials

What you need:

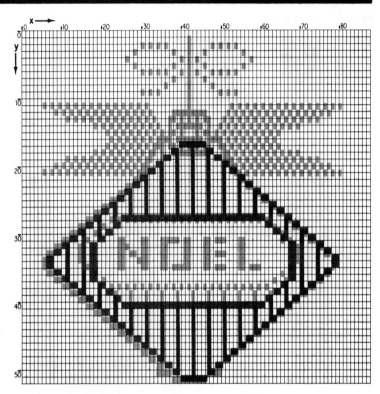

Before & After:

(*Noel*)

Ideas:

The "Noel" Christmas ornament graphic can be turned into a crest. Initials can be added to the open space with the Graphic Editor and saved on disk. Initials can also be added in the text mode, but be sure to roll back the paper to the appropriate starting position. If you have a set of templates (see pages 000-000) you can plan more easily. You can also print the crest and add initials or words by hand...as suggested in the seating assignment chart. The crest is ideal for personalized stationery.

Applications:

See page 43.

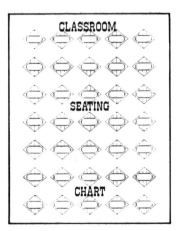

Paperdoll

What you need:

Before & After:

(*Winner*)

Ideas:

Paperdolls made with *The Print Shop* are fun because you can create your own clothes and color them as you wish. Printing out several of the same creations and coloring each one differently adds fun time without more computer effort. For quicker results, create the clothes and use the "Winner" as is.

Applications:

See page 81.

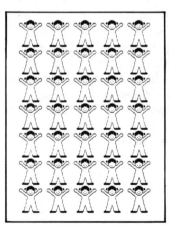

Paperdoll Clothes-1

What you need:

Before & After:

(*Winner*)

Ideas:

The ideas for clothes for the "Winner" paperdoll are only as limited as your time and imagination. Starting with the "Winner" you can erase the minimum amount of the doll and save that graphic to create numerous outfits with arms.

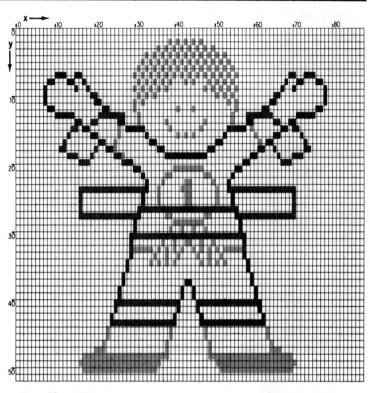

Applications:

Paperdoll Clothes-2

What you need:

Before & After:

(Winner)

Ideas:

Clothes without arms for the "Winner" paperdoll can be created by saving a shell graphic first. From that graphic many different outfits can be drawn easily. Print the doll and the clothes in the sign mode choosing the medium-sized graphic staggered for five of the same graphic. For variety, color in each graphic differently. Or print one large doll in the sign mode and one large set of clothes.

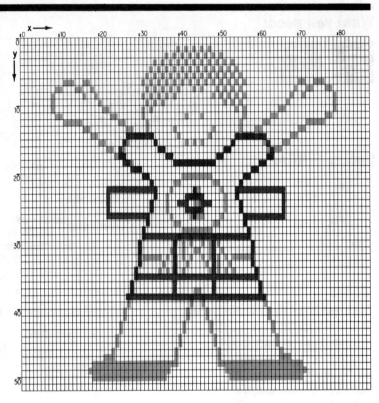

Applications:

Plane

What you need:

Before & After:

(*Plane*)

Ideas:

Turn an illustrative type
graphic into a logo by simply
erasing the decorative sky
and filling in the plane. In
addition to a logo or
background pattern, the
plane can be used for any
travel-related message.

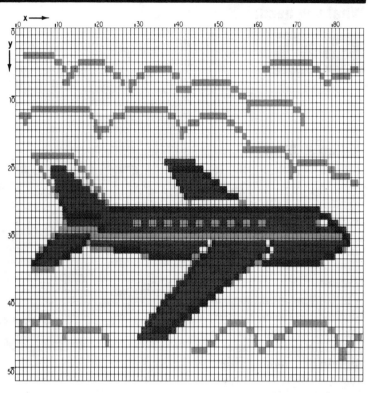

Applications:

See page 80.

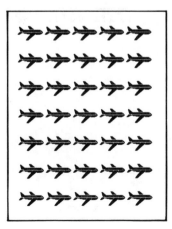

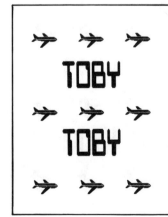

Rocker

What you need:

Before & After:

(*Rocker*)

Ideas:

A little filling in and some art touch-up (as the ears) make this "Rocker" graphic a nice symbol for any business or organization working with young children. It also is an ideal symbol for a child's personalized stationery or greeting card.

Applications:

See page 80.

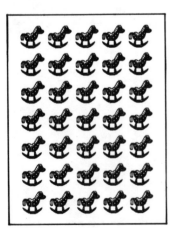

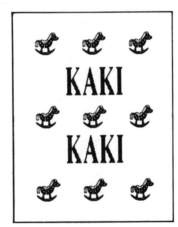

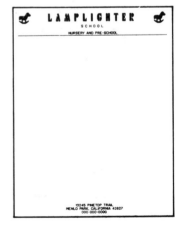

School

What you need:

Before & After:

(*School*)

Ideas:

A "cute" drawing can become a symbol when some detail is erased and the graphic is strengthened by blackening in the interior. A more generic "building" look can be accomplished by erasing the flag, bell and the window details of the shades.

Applications:

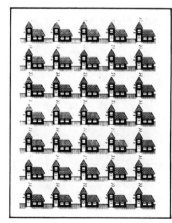

Tree

What you need:

Before & After:

(*Park*)

Ideas:

The Print Shop's "Park" graphic is well suited for a logo when the grass is erased and the trunk is made straighter. You may not want to take the time to clean up the interior of the tree. The grass and trunk work alone will help make the tree a stronger graphic.

Applications:
See page 115.

Arrow

What you need:

Before & After:

(Mason)

Ideas:

The arrow is in place when you choose the "Mason" graphic. Only the handle is touched up. Use this art as original art if you don't yet own the Graphics Library 2 (IBM/Graphics Library 1). Try turning the page over and holding it up to the light if you need a right pointing arrow and enter in the Graphics Editor as an original graphic.

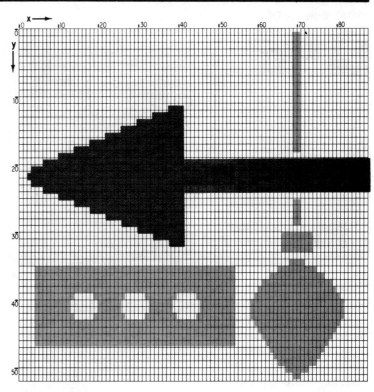

Applications:

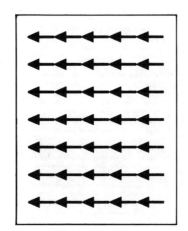 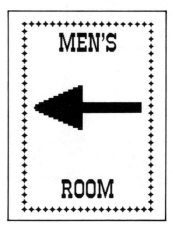

Design 5

What you need:

Before & After:

(*Easter*)

Ideas:

Many Print Shop graphics become something new when you look at them long enough. Try making this "Easter" egg into a new creation by extending the design and erasing the curved edge of the egg. The "Easter" graphic also provides a nice oval frame for another graphic idea. Just erase the interior, keeping the border, and add letters or graphics.

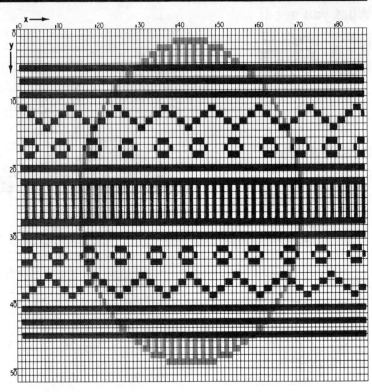

Applications:

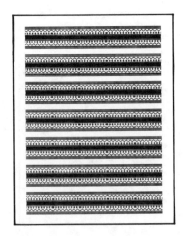 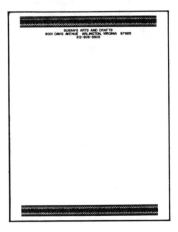

Design 6

What you need:

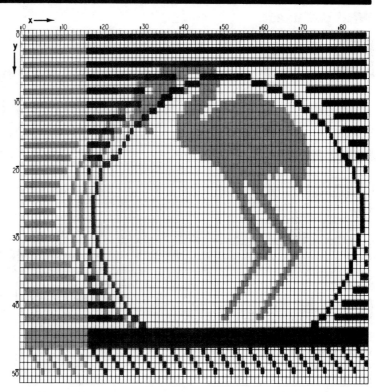

Before & After:

(Flamingo)

Ideas:

Make a crest for initials or other graphic insert by erasing the flamingo, patching the circle where its head was and erasing the far left side so that the semi-circle frame is symmetrical. The striped background can also be blackened in for a crisper, more professional look.

Applications:

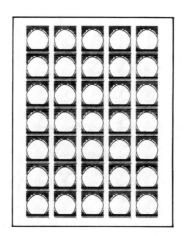 

Design 7

What you need:

Before & After:

(*Soccer*)

Ideas:

A "Soccer" ball holds interesting patterns. Here a strong statement is made with a triangular logo. Another design can be made by filling in the three "balls" and outlining only the triangle bars.

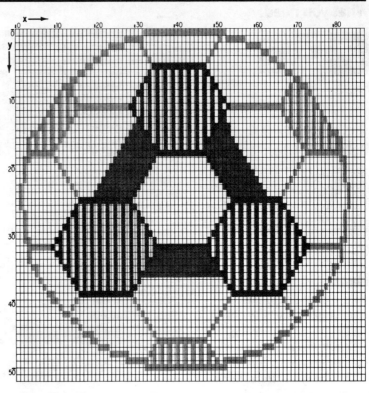

Applications:

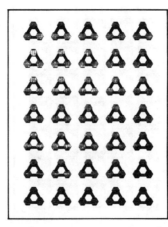

Dollar

What you need:

Before & After:

(Dollar)

Ideas:

The outlined "Dollar" sign becomes a bold and professional symbol when the surrounding Graphic Editor box is filled in. Note how well solid black boxes work in repetition as they form a new graphic by butting up to one another.

Applications:

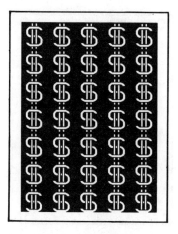  

Figures

What you need:

Before & After:

(Jewel)

Ideas:

This "Jewel" graphic is transformed into a figurative symbol with the addition of two heads, a little clean up and two sections filled in. The generic look of this symbol is appropriate for more than romantic communications. Skating rinks or classes, dance schools, and announcements of recitals are examples of applications.

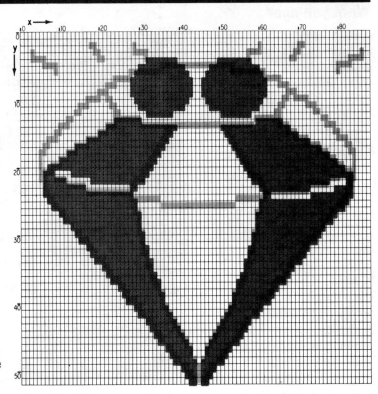

Applications:

Circle Design

What you need:

*(App/
Comm only)*

Before & After:

(Life Buoy)

Ideas:

The simplified "Life Buoy" can be used as a nautical looking logo. It can be simplified further by filling in the entire circle. Try drawing a cross through the center for a still different design… either with or without the shape filled in.

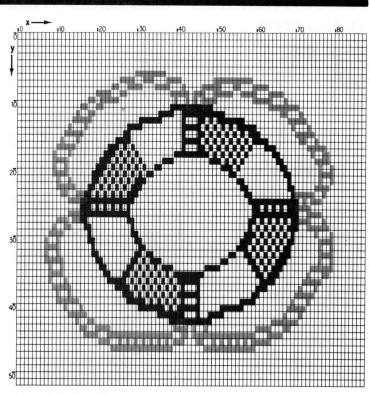

Applications:

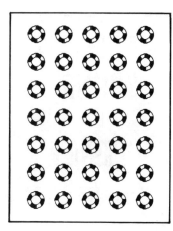

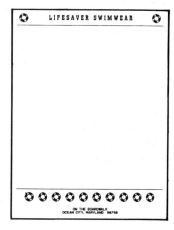

Grid

What you need:

Before & After:

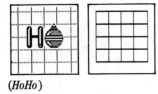

(*HoHo*)

Ideas:

A grid is a good basic design element which can be used in infinite ways. By starting with the "HoHo" graphic from the Graphics Library 3 (IBM/ Graphics Library 2), you can avoid some counting in the Graphic Editor. Try filling in every other square in a checkerboard manner for a bolder look. This makes a great background pattern in the sign mode choosing small, tiled graphic. Also, try printing in the Graphic Editor down the left side repeatedly. (Just choose "PRINT," don't roll your paper and keep printing until you have a complete column.)

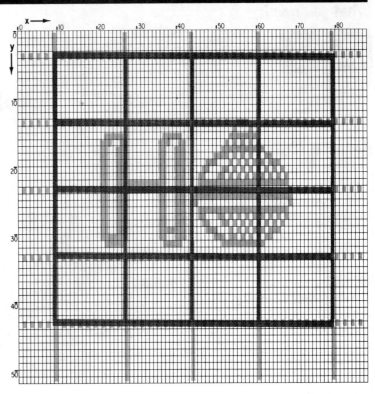

Applications:

Pointing Finger

What you need:

(App/ Comm only)

Before & After:

(Thumbs Up)

Ideas:

The "Thumbs Up" graphic makes an excellent pointing finger symbol when modified. It is adaptable to many applications. For a left pointing finger, copy this page, then turn it over and hold it up to the light.

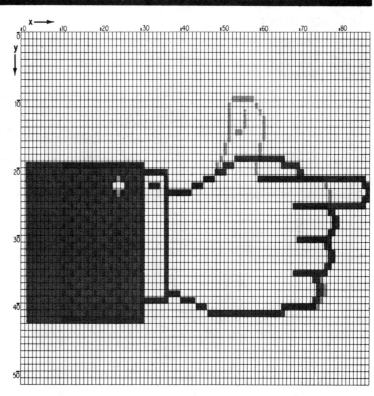

Applications:

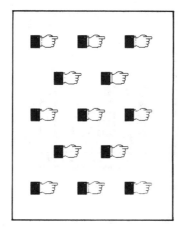

Shadow Box

What you need:

(App/ Comm only)

Before & After:

(File)

Ideas:

With a little erasing and adding, the "File" graphic can become an interesting box for adding other art or letters. Printed large, it can make a fun frame for children to draw in. Print in the medium size and add letters or rub-on type for your initials.

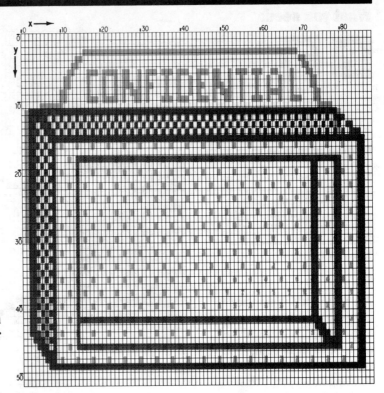

Applications:

Triangle

What you need:

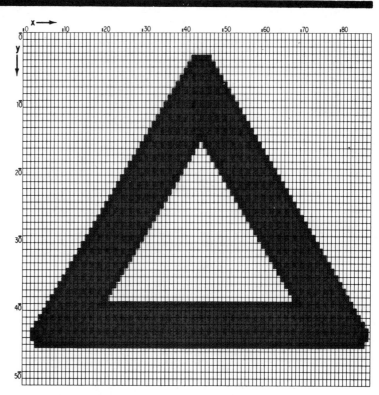

Before & After:

(*Warning*)

Ideas:

A triangle, as a logo element, communicates strength and unity. It also is a simple decorative element alone or in repetition for a new design or as a background pattern. The triangle here is easy to create…just fill in the Print Shop "Warning" graphic.

Applications:

Planning Tools

■ FONT CATEGORIES

■ TEMPLATE CHARTS

■ SAMPLE TEMPLATES

■ THE FONTS

■ GRAPHIC SPECIFICATIONS

■ ABOUT THE ART GRID

What's in This Section

This section is a collection of tools to use when you're working on an original Print Shop creation. There are easy-to-create tools that show you Print Shop layout possibilities, help you plan and organize your design ideas, allow you to control and predict where in a design your graphics and text will sit. With the planning tools at your side, you'll be able to fine tune your design before you even turn on your computer.

Highlighted for you here is an overview of what you'll find in this section.

The Templates: You'll find templates or "design models" you can easily create that show where on a page your graphics and text will appear–before you print!

The Graphics: You'll find every graphic from *The Print Shop* program, *Graphics Library 1, Graphics Library 2, Graphics Library 3* (Apple and Commodore), and *Holiday Edition* marked for size to be used together with the templates.

The Art Grid: You'll find a blank grid to copy and use for your own original graphics.

Using This Section

When you're working on an original Print Shop design, remember the planning tools. Use them to find the layout that works best for the message you want to convey. Use them to determine the right size and position for your pictures and words. Use them to eliminate guesswork—know in advance the outcome of your design choices. Use the planning tools to save time and paper!

Highlighted for you here (and first introduced and explained on pages 8-9) are suggestions for approaching this section and getting the most mileage out of the planning tools.

SUGGESTION #1: Put the templates to work for you! They're invaluable guides for determining where to place pictures and words on the page.

SUGGESTION #2: Consider the height of a graphic when you plan your design. Some designs work better with a tall graphic, others work best with a shorter one. Use the Graphic Specifications section to find the height of the graphic you want to use. (You can also use this section in place of the Graphics Card to preview all the graphics available to you.)

SUGGESTION #3: Plan ahead! Use the tools to organize your thoughts before you even boot up your disk.

SUGGESTION #4: When you're thinking of a new design idea, look at the patterns created by the placement of graphics and text as shown in a template. The pattern possibilities may trigger ideas. (Remember, in the greeting card and sign modes there's a custom option with small- and medium-sized graphics that lets you individually select the position(s) you want to use from the staggered pattern.)

SUGGESTION #5: Try creative layouts. For example, alternate rows of text with rows of graphics. Place all your graphics at the left and your words at the right. With the planning tools nearby, being more creative is easy!

Getting to Know the Templates

When you're planning a new Print Shop design, call on the templates. These powerful tools are "design models"–they show where on a page graphics and text will appear. Templates are easy to create and can be used again and again to plan your designs. Templates are particularly valuable for the greeting card, sign and letterhead modes. Because banner layouts are so easy to plan, templates are not necessary.

So, when you're about to create a sign, a card or a letterhead, and you don't want your pictures and words to overlap, just consult the appropriate template. You'll know exactly where to place your pictures and words if you don't want them to meet on the page– and where to place them if you do.

A Sample Template

The sample sign/card template shown here highlights for you the various template elements. (For additional samples, see pages 236-252.)

Template Boxes: Represent the positions of graphics. Markings within a box indicate different graphic heights (see Working Together, page 226).

Side Letters: Show the position of each line of text and the number of lines per page for that font category. (Hint: Use a ruler, or other straightedged object, to follow where the line extends across the page.)

Top Row Letters: Show the approximate number of letters per line for that font (for all fonts, see pages 254-267).

Graphic: Medium – Graphic size (available only for signs and cards)

Staggered – Graphic layout

Font: News – Font category (see Font Categories, pages 228-231).

Small – Font size (available only for signs and cards)

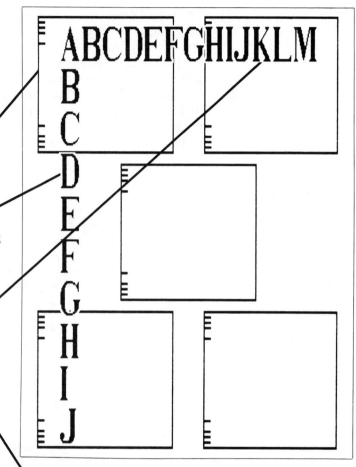

GRAPHIC: MEDIUM/STAGGERED
FONT: NEWS/SMALL

A Sample Design

The sample design shown here was created using the sample sign/ card template on the previous page as a guide. Notice the position of graphics and text in the sign. The pictures clear the words. Notice the position of graphics and identical text lines in the template. The graphics clear the text there, too! The template was used as a "design model" or guide to create the sign. The template allowed the designer to know in advance where the graphics and text would sit in the sign. It allowed the designer to know in advance that the pictures and words of this sign would not overlap on the printed page!

YOU ARE MY
SUNSHINE
LAURA

I
LOVE
YOU!

Here's another sample design that was created using the same template.

Creating A Template

Creating a template is easy! In fact, it's so easy you may want to create your own personal template file of the fonts and graphic patterns you use most frequently—or even a complete set with all possible combinations of fonts and graphics. (To create a complete set of templates just use the charts on pages 231-234 as a guide.) In this way, you can consult the appropriate template whenever you're ready to work on an original Print Shop design.

**First:
Choose a Graphic**

The first step in creating a template is to consider the graphic. The graphic shown below is the recommended graphic to use.

The *template box* is the graphic used in all the handbook templates. The New Art section shows you how to create the box (see page 172). Use the Graphic Editor and input this graphic—ahead of time—just as you would any piece of original art. It takes less than five minutes! Then save the box on disk, and call it up as your graphic whenever you create a new template. (See more about the template box on pages 226-227.)

**Two Groups of
Templates**

The Print Shop templates can be divided into two groups: SIGN/CARD and LETTERHEAD.

The greeting card and sign modes of *The Print Shop* offer the exact same choices for the placement of graphics and text. The front of a greeting card and a sign are 100% interchangeable. The only difference is the size in which the design prints. (This point is useful to remember when you're looking for a card or sign idea in Designs, Designs, Designs.) Because the graphic and text positions for the card and sign modes are identical, one set of templates works for both! You may prefer using the sign mode because of its larger size. A separate set of templates is required for the letterhead mode.

Creating A Sign/Card Template: Step-by-Step

To create a sign/card template:

1. Choose your mode: SIGN or CARD—they're interchangeable!

2. Choose DESIGN YOUR OWN.

3. Choose a border. Select NO BORDER unless, of course, you want to see where a particular border sits on the page relative to the text and graphics.

4. Choose your graphic. The Template Box on page 172 is recommended. (An alternative of similar shape and size is Graphic 34 on *The Print Shop* program disk.)

5. Choose your graphic size: SMALL, MEDIUM or LARGE.

6. Choose your graphic layout. STAGGERED or TILED for small- and medium-sized graphics, no option for large graphics.

7. Choose a font. For Apple and Commodore—Alexia, News, Stencil can be used to represent all fonts. For IBM—Alexia, News, Starlet, Deco, Block, Typewriter, Stencil can be used to represent all fonts. (See About The Font Categories, pages 228-229.)

8. Choose a font size: SMALL or LARGE (Note: Font size must be selected separately for each line.)

9. Enter your text. Follow the handbook templates:
    *Starting in the LEFT position, type a letter in every available position across the top line.
    *Type one letter in the LEFT position of each row down the side.

10. You're ready to print! Save your printed template in a template file to use over and over again!

Creating A Letterhead Template: Step-by-Step

To create a letterhead template:

1. Choose your mode: LETTERHEAD.

2. Choose DESIGN YOUR OWN.

3. Choose your graphic: The Template Box on page 172 is recommended. (An alternative of similar shape and size is Graphic 34 on *The Print Shop* program disk.)

4. Choose your graphic position. LEFT CORNER, RIGHT CORNER, BOTH, ROW OF SIX or TILED.

5. Choose your font. For Apple and Commodore–Alexia, News, Stencil can be used to represent all fonts. For IBM–Alexia, News, Starlet, Deco, Block, Typewriter, Stencil can be used to represent all fonts. (See About The Font Categories, pages 228-229.)

6. Enter your text. Follow the handbook templates:
   *Type a letter in every available position on the name line.
   *Type a letter in every available position on each address line.
(In this way you'll know how many letters can fit on each line!)

7. You're ready to print! Save your printed template in a template file to use over and over again!

Using A Template

Templates are easy to create and so easy to use! They'll help you determine the position of your words. And the position of your graphics. Here's how to use a template.

Positioning Your Words

The sample handbook templates show letters positioned two ways— in a row that runs across the top line and in a row that runs from top to bottom down the left-hand side of the page.

The row that runs across the top line shows the approximate number of letters that fit on a line for that particular font. This number may vary slightly depending on the width of the actual letters you select. Pages 253-267 show approximately how many letters fit on a line for every font on the Print Shop program disk. Apple, Commodore and IBM fonts are grouped separately.

The row of letters that runs down the left-hand side of a template shows where each line of text falls on the page. It shows where text sits relative to graphics. To follow the line across the page, use a ruler or other straightedged object as a guide.

Positioning Your Graphics

THE TEMPLATE BOXES

Within the handbook's sample templates are boxes that show the position of graphics. The outline of each template box shows how much space the *largest possible graphic* occupies and where it sits on the page. (The template box can be copied and used for your own templates. Just follow the pattern shown on page 172.)

Most Print Shop graphics are not as large as the template box. Some are narrower and many are shorter. This latter information, how short or tall a graphic is, may be key to many of your designs. Often a shorter graphic can clear an extra line (or two!) of text. It may be just what you need to complete a message and to fit in all your words.

How do you know how tall a graphic is? How do you know how much space it will occupy? Just turn to Graphic Specifications—a companion to the templates.

Working Together

TEMPLATE BOXES AND GRAPHIC SPECIFICATIONS

The Graphic Specifications section shows every graphic marked for size from *The Print Shop* program disk, *Graphics Library 1*, *Graphics Library 2*, *Graphics Library 3* (Apple and Commodore), and *Holiday Edition*. Apple and Commodore graphics are grouped together and IBM graphics are grouped separately. Every graphic, like the one shown here is marked with two numbers.

(2.49)

The numbers indicate how many lines from the top and bottom of the template box the graphic will sit. The template box is marked with lines at the left. The lines represent line numbers.

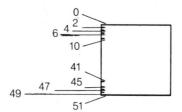

Match the numbers from a graphic with the line numbers of the template box as shown in the following examples:

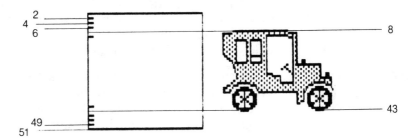

You'll know where that graphic will appear in a template. You'll know whether the graphic will hit a line of text or clear it. You'll know just how tall your graphic will be in your design–before you print!

Notice that the top line of the template box is labeled 0, the bottom line is labeled 51. (These numbers are the y-coordinates from the Graphic Editor. For more about the Graphic Editor coordinates, see page 144.) A graphic labeled 0 at top and 51 at bottom is the same height as the template box. A graphic labeled 0 and 51 is the tallest possible graphic. A graphic labeled 1 and 50 is slightly shorter. A graphic labeled 2 and 49 is even shorter, and so on.

Use a template to see if your design requires a tall graphic. Or a shorter graphic. You may find that a taller or shorter graphic is not absolutely necessary, but could improve the look of your design by allowing more space, or less space, between your pictures and words. Then head for the Graphic Specifications section to find a graphic that fits your design!

About the Font Categories

When you create a template with one font, or text style, it's likely you'll be able to use that same template to plan designs with a different font. (How convenient!) *The Print Shop* fonts can be divided into categories by size. The fonts within each category allow the same number of lines per page. Create a set of templates with one font and use the same templates to plan designs with other fonts from the same font category.

For Apple and Commodore Users

The Print Shop offers Apple and Commodore users eight unique fonts (see The Fonts, pages 253-259). The Apple and Commodore fonts can be divided into three categories as shown below. The number of lines per page for the small and large sizes of each font are also shown.

Category 1 –	(Small: 8 lines)	Alexia
	(Large: 4 lines)	RSVP
Category 2 –	(Small: 10 lines)	News
	(Large: 5 lines)	Tech
		Party
Category 3 –	(Small: 14 lines)	Stencil
	(Large: 7 lines)	Block
		Typewriter

Alexia, News and Stencil can be used in Apple and Commodore templates to represent the three font categories. So, for example, if you want to plan a design with RSVP, you can use the Alexia templates. You can use the News templates for Tech and Party, and the Stencil templates for Block and Typewriter. Each font within the same category has the same number of lines per page. (Keep in mind, however, the number of letters per line varies between font styles and in fact, may vary slightly for the same font, depending on the width of the letters you choose. To see approximately how many letters fit across a line for each font, see pages 254-259.)

For IBM Users

The Print Shop offers IBM users 12 unique fonts (see The Fonts, pages 260-267). The IBM fonts can be divided into seven categories as shown below. The number of lines per page for the small and large sizes of each font are also shown.

Category 1 –	(Small: 8 lines)	Alexia
	(Large: 4 lines)	RSVP
		Thames
Category 2 –	(Small: 9 lines)	News
	(Large: 4.5 lines)	Tech
		Party
Category 3 –	(Small: 10 lines)	Starlet
	(Large: 5 lines)	
Category 4 –	(Small: 11 lines)	Deco
	(Large: 5.5 lines)	
Category 5 –	(Small: 12 lines)	Block
	(Large: 6 lines)	
Category 6 –	(Small: 13 lines)	Typewriter
	(Large: 6.5 lines)	
Category 7 –	(Small: 14 lines)	Stencil
	(Large: 7 lines)	Reporter

Alexia, News, Starlet, Deco, Block, Typewriter, and Stencil can be used in IBM templates to represent the seven font categories. So, for example, if you want to plan a design with Thames, you can use the templates with Alexia. You can use the templates with News for Tech and Party, and the templates with Stencil for Reporter. Each font within the same category has the same number of lines per page. (Keep in mind that the number of letters per line varies between fonts – and may even vary within the same font depending on the width of the letters you select. To see approximately how many letters fit across a line for each font, see pages 260-267.)

Templates — A Complete Set

The templates are so helpful—and addictive—you may find yourself (like us!) wanting a complete set to use for *all* your original Print Shop design work. The template layout chart will help you organize the pieces.

The template layout chart describes every component in a complete set of Apple and Commodore templates and every component in a complete set of IBM templates. Each font represents a font category. For your own templates, use the font shown or substitute another font from the same category. (See About The Font Categories, pages 228-229.)

Apple/Commodore Sign-Card Templates

Template #	Graphic size	Layout	Font	Font size
1	S	stagger	alexia	S
2	S	stagger	alexia	L
3	S	stagger	news	S
4	S	stagger	news	L
5	S	stagger	stencil	S
6	S	stagger	stencil	L
7	S	tile	alexia	S
8	S	tile	alexia	L
9	S	tile	news	S
10	S	tile	news	L
11	S	tile	stencil	S
12	S	tile	stencil	L
13	M	stagger	alexia	S
14	M	stagger	alexia	L
15	M	stagger	news	S
16	M	stagger	news	L
17	M	stagger	stencil	S
18	M	stagger	stencil	L
19	L	n/a	alexia	S
20	L	n/a	alexia	L
21	L	n/a	news	S
22	L	n/a	news	L
23	L	n/a	stencil	S
24	L	n/a	stencil	L

Apple/Commodore Letterhead Templates

Template #	Position	Font
1	both	alexia
2	both	news
3	both	stencil
4	row of six	alexia
5	row of six	news
6	row of six	stencil
7	tiled	alexia
8	tiled	news
9	tiled	stencil

Templates with BOTH show the LEFT CORNER and RIGHT CORNER positions. Therefore, to see all three positions, create one set of templates with BOTH.

IBM Sign-Card Templates

Template #	Graphic size	Layout	Font	Font size
1	S	stagger	alexia	S
2	S	stagger	alexia	L
3	S	stagger	news	S
4	S	stagger	news	L
5	S	stagger	starlet	S
6	S	stagger	starlet	L
7	S	stagger	deco	S
8	S	stagger	deco	L
9	S	stagger	block	S
10	S	stagger	block	L
11	S	stagger	typewriter	S
12	S	stagger	typewriter	L
13	S	stagger	stencil	S
14	S	stagger	stencil	L
15	S	tile	alexia	S
16	S	tile	alexia	L
17	S	tile	news	S
18	S	tile	news	L
19	S	tile	starlet	S
20	S	tile	starlet	L
21	S	tile	deco	S
22	S	tile	deco	L
23	S	tile	block	S
24	S	tile	block	L

(Continued on next page)

Template #	Graphic size	Layout	Font	Font size
25	S	tile	typewriter	S
26	S	tile	typewriter	L
27	S	tile	stencil	S
28	S	tile	stencil	L
29	M	stagger	alexia	S
30	M	stagger	alexia	L
31	M	stagger	news	S
32	M	stagger	news	L
33	M	stagger	stencil	S
34	M	stagger	stencil	L
35	L	n/a	alexia	S
36	L	n/a	alexia	L
37	L	n/a	news	S
38	L	n/a	news	L
39	L	n/a	starlet	S
40	L	n/a	starlet	L
41	L	n/a	deco	S
42	L	n/a	deco	L
43	L	n/a	block	S
44	L	n/a	block	L
45	L	n/a	typewriter	S
46	L	n/a	typewriter	L
47	L	n/a	stencil	S
48	L	n/a	stencil	L

IBM Letterhead Templates

Template #	Position	Font
1	both	alexia
2	both	news
3	both	starlet
4	both	deco
5	both	block
6	both	typewriter
7	both	stencil
8	row of six	alexia
9	row of six	news
10	row of six	starlet
11	row of six	deco
12	row of six	block
13	row of six	typewriter
14	row of six	stencil
15	tiled	alexia
16	tiled	news
17	tiled	starlet
18	tiled	deco
19	tiled	block
20	tiled	typewriter
21	tiled	stencil

Templates with BOTH show the LEFT CORNER and RIGHT CORNER positions. Therefore, to see all three positions, create one set of templates with BOTH.

More Sample Templates

To see the breadth and variety of template patterns (and their value), flip through the handbook samples. Two sets are included organized by font and graphic size.

By Font. A complete set of Alexia templates shows the font with every possible graphic size and pattern. Notice where the various graphic sizes and patterns clear the text lines and where they don't. A similar set of templates can be created for a font you frequently use.

By Graphic Size: A complete set of templates with the medium-sized graphic shows the graphic with each of the three Apple and Commodore font categories. Notice which fonts allow you to clear the most or fewest lines of text. A similar set of templates can be created for a graphic size or pattern you frequently use.

Note: The handbook templates were created on an Apple computer with an ImageWriter printer. Templates created with a different configuration or system may vary slightly. To assure accuracy, create your templates on the same system you use to create your Print Shop designs.

Templates With Alexia Font

Sign-Card

GRAPHIC: SMALL/STAGGERED
FONT: ALEXIA/SMALL

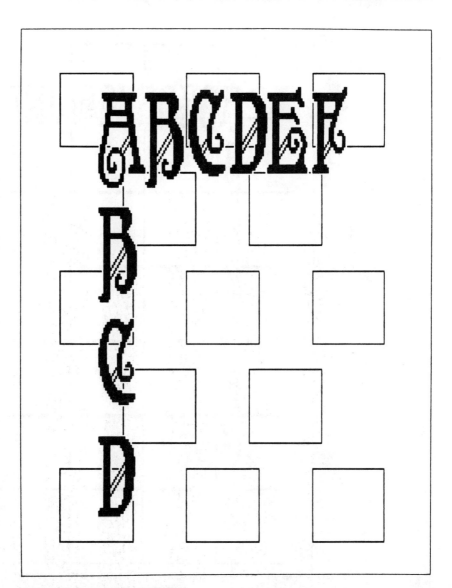

GRAPHIC: SMALL/STAGGERED
FONT: ALEXIA/LARGE

ABCDEFGHIJKLM

B
C
D
E
F
G
H

GRAPHIC: SMALL/TILED
FONT: ALEXIA/SMALL

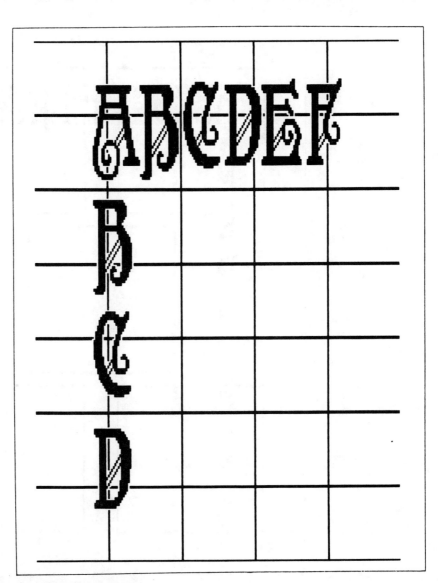

GRAPHIC: SMALL/TILED
FONT: ALEXIA/LARGE

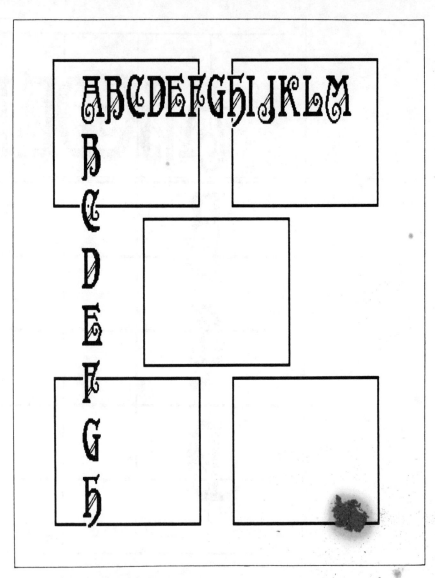

GRAPHIC: MEDIUM/STAGGERED
FONT: ALEXIA/SMALL

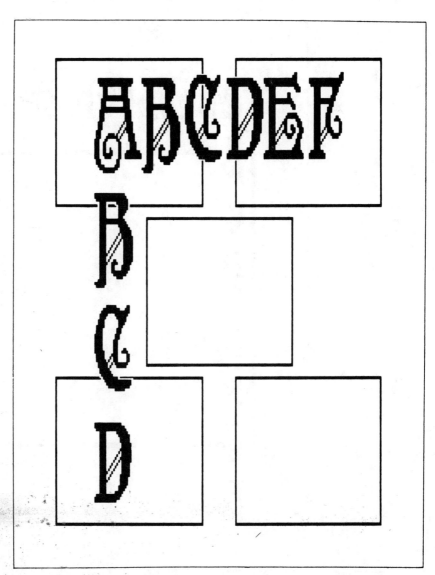

GRAPHIC: MEDIUM/STAGGERED
FONT: ALEXIA/LARGE

ABCDEFGHIJKLM

B
C
D
E
F
G
H

GRAPHIC: LARGE
FONT: ALEXIA/SMALL

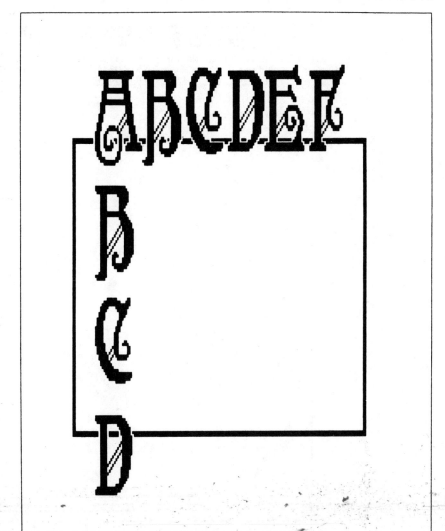

GRAPHIC: LARGE
FONT: ALEXIA/LARGE

Letterhead

ABCDEFGHIJKLMNOPQRSTUVWXYZ123

ABCDEFGHIJKLMNOPQRSTUVWXYZ1234567890ABCDEFGHIJKLMNOPQRSTU
ABCDEFGHIJKLMNOPQRSTUVWXYZ1234567890ABCDEFGHIJKLMNOPQRTSU
ABCDEFGHIJKLMNOPQRSTUVWXYZ1234567890ABCDEFGHIJKLMNOPQRSTU

GRAPHIC: BOTH CORNERS
FONT: ALEXIA

ABCDEFGHIJKLMNOPQRSTUVWXYZ123

ABCDEFGHIJKLMNOPQRSTUVWXYZ1234567890ABCDEFGHIJKLMNOPQRSTU
ABCDEFGHIJKLMNOPQRSTUVWXYZ1234567890ABCDEFGHIJKLMNOPQRSTU
ABCDEFGHIJKLMNOPQRSTUVWXYZ1234567890ABCDEFGHIJKLMNOPQRSTU

GRAPHIC: ROW OF SIX
FONT: ALEXIA

ABCDEFGHIJKLMNOPQRSTUVWXYZ123

ABCDEFGHIJKLMNOPQRSTUVWXYZ1234567890ABCDEFGHIJKLMNOPQRSTU
ABCDEFGHIJKLMNOPQRSTUVWXYZ1234567890ABCDEFGHIJKLMNOPORTSU
ABCDEFGHIJKLMNOPQRSTUVWXYZ1234567890ABCDEFGHIJKLMNOPQRSTU

GRAPHIC: TILED
FONT: ALEXIA

Templates With Medium Graphics

Sign-Card

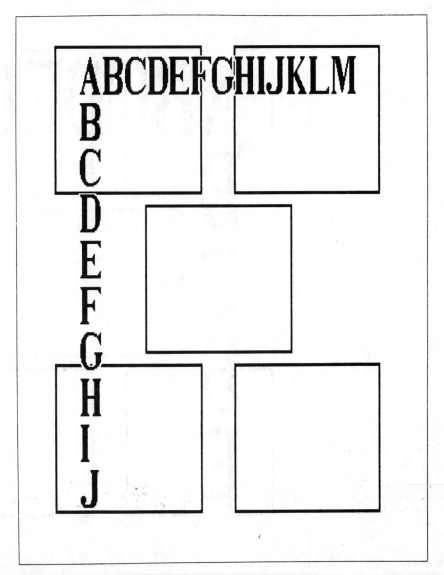

GRAPHIC: MEDIUM/STAGGERED
FONT: NEWS/SMALL

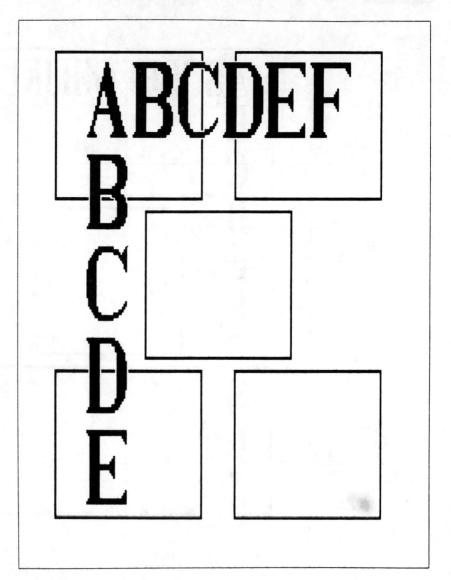

GRAPHIC: MEDIUM/STAGGERED
FONT: NEWS/LARGE

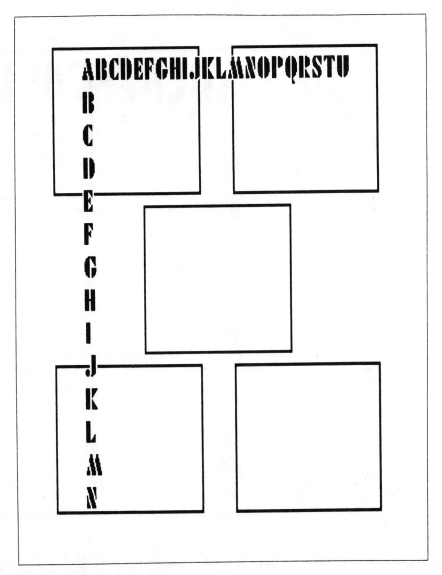

GRAPHIC: MEDIUM/STAGGERED
FONT: STENCIL/SMALL

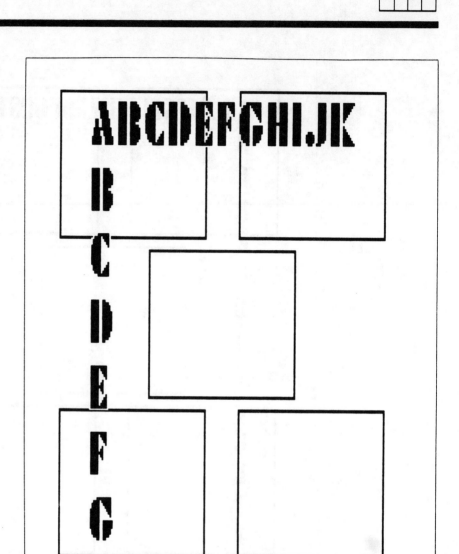

GRAPHIC: MEDIUM/STAGGERED
FONT: STENCIL/LARGE

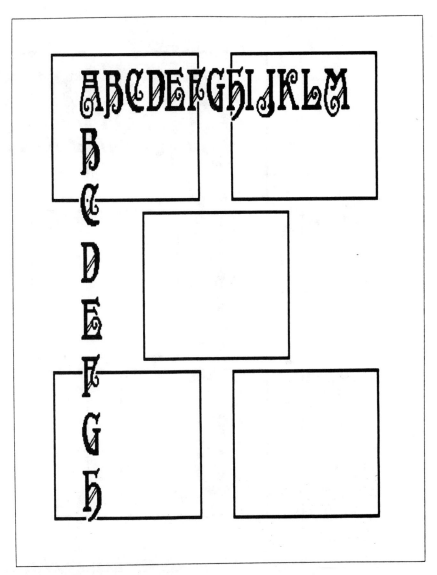

GRAPHIC: MEDIUM/STAGGERED
FONT: ALEXIA/SMALL

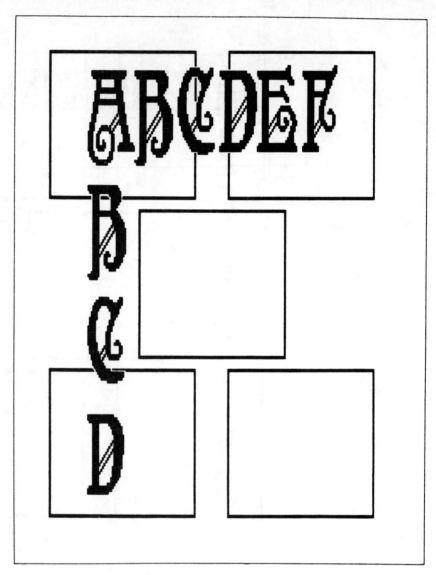

GRAPHIC: MEDIUM/STAGGERED
FONT: ALEXIA/LARGE

The Fonts

Each font, or text style, allows you to type a certain number of letters per line. The *approximate* number of letters that fit on a line, starting from the LEFT position, is shown here for all Print Shop program fonts. Fonts for Apple, Commodore, and IBM are shown separately. It is important to note that the number of letters that fit on a line for each font may vary slightly depending on the width of the actual letters you select. For example, if your words have many narrow letters such as *i*'s and *l*'s, you may fit more letters on a line. If your words have many wide letters such as *m*'s and *w*'s, you may fit fewer on a line.

Apple Fonts

RSVP

Small

ABCDEFGHIJKL

ABCDE

Large

ALEXIA

Small

ABCDEFGHIJKLM

ABCDEF

Large

NEWS

Small

ABCDEFGHIJKLM

ABCDEF

Large

TECH

Small

ABCDEFGHIJKLMN

Large

ABCDEFG

PARTY

Small

ABCDEFGHIJKLMN

Large

ABCDEFG

BLOCK
Small

ABCDEFGHIJKLMNOP

Large

ABCDEFGH

STENCIL
Small

ABCDEFGHIJKLMNOPQRSTU

Large

ABCDEFGHIJK

TYPEWRITER
Small

ABCDEFGHIJKLMNOPQRSTU

Large

ABCDEFGHIJK

Commodore Fonts

RSVP

Small

ABCDEFGHIJKLM

Large

ABCDEF

ALEXIA

Small

ABCDEFGHIJKLMNO

Large

ABCDEFG

NEWS

Small

ABCDEFGHIJKLMNO

Large

ABCDEFG

TECH

Small

ABCDEFGHIJKLMNOP

Large

ABCDEFGHI

PARTY

Small

ABCDEFGHIJKLMNOP

Large

ABCDEFGHI

BLOCK
Small

ABCDEFGHIJKLMNOPQR

Large

ABCDEFGHIJ

STENCIL
Small

ABCDEFGHIJKLMNOPQRSTUVW

Large

ABCDEFGHIJKL

TYPEWRITER
Small

ABCDEFGHIJKLMNOPQRSTUVW

Large

ABCDEFGHIJKL

IBM Fonts

THAMES

Small

ABCDEFGH

abcdefghi

Large

ABCD

abcd

RSVP

Small

ABCDEFGHIJKLM

abcdefghijklmn

Large

ABCDEF

abcdefg

ALEXIA

Small

ABCDEFGHI JKLMNO

abcdefghijklmnop

Large

ABCDEFG

abcdefgh

NEWS

Small

ABCDEFGHIJKLMN

abcdefghijklmno

Large

ABCDEFG

abcdefg

TECH

Small

ABCDEFGHIJKLMNO

abcdefghijklmnopq

Large

ABCDEFGH
abcdefghi

DECO
Small

ABCDEFGHIJKLMN

abcdefghijklmno

Large

ABCDEFG

abcdefg

PARTY

Small

ABCDEFGHIJKLMNO

ABCDEFGHIJKLMNOPQ

Large

ABCDEFGH

ABCDEFGHI

BLOCK
Small

ABCDEFGHIJKLMNOPQR

abcdefghijklmnopqrst

Large

ABCDEFGHIJ

abcdefghij

STARLET
Small

ABCDEFGHIJKLMN

abcdefghijklmno

Large

ABCDEFG

abcdefg

REPORTER
Small

ABCDEFGHIJKLMNOPQRSTUVW

abcdefghijklmnopqrstuvwxy

Large

ABCDEFGHIJKL

abcdefghijklm

TYPEWRITER
Small

ABCDEFGHIJKLMNOPQRSTUVWX

abcdefghijklmnopqrstuvwxy

Large

ABCDEFGHIJKL

abcdefghijklm

STENCIL
Small

ABCDEFGHIJKLMNOPQRSTUVW

abcdefghijklmnopqrstuvwxy

Large

ABCDEFGHIJKL

abcdefghijklm

Apple/Commodore Graphic Specifications

Program Disk

1 (4,48)   10 (4,48)   19 (2,49)   28 (8,43)   37 (1,48)   46 (2,49)   54 (0,51)

2 (5,47)   11 (1,50)   20 (2,50)   29 (8,44)   38 (4,48)   47 (1,49)   55 (0,51)

3 (3,45)   12 (3,49)   21 (1,50)   30 (1,49)   39 (1,51)   48 (10,41)   56 (0,51)

4 (5,46)   13 (0,51)*   22 (3,48)   31 (2,50)   40 (5,47)   49 (5,46)   57 (0,51)

5 (5,47)   14 (6,46)   23 (18,40)   32 (4,46)   41 (1,51)   50 (6,44)   57 (0,51)

6 (1,51)   15 (5,44)   24 (2,50)   33 (5,46)   42 (5,45)   51 (0,51)   58 (0,51)

7 (0,47)   16 (4,48)   25 (1,50)   34 (2,50)   43 (2,50)   52 (0,51)   59 (1,51)

8 (3,47)   17 (1,51)   26 (1,51)   35 (1,50)   44 (2,47)   53 (0,51)   60 (0,51)

9 (5,50)   18 (0,50)   27 (5,46)   36 (1,50)   45 (4,45)

*Apple only

Graphics Library 1

FIRE (0,51)	ANGEL (4,47)	STOCKING (1,50)	CAROL (0,51)	MANGER (4,47)	RUDOLPH (1,50)	COOKIES* (2,49)	TREE (1,50)
SNOWMAN (2,49)	SNOWGIRL* (0,51)	HOME (1,50)	MAMA (1,50)	JUNIOR (0,50)	PAPA (1,50)	DREIDEL (1,50)	HOLLY* (1,51)
SANTA (0,51)	SLED* (0,51)	CANE (0,50)	NOEL (0,51)	PARTY* (0,51)	PARTY 2*	GROUNDHOG (2,51)	PATRICK (0,51)
BUNNY (0,51)	CHICK (2,49)	FLOWERS* (0,51)	DUCK (0,51)	FLAG (1,50)	CHEF (0,51)	PICNIC (0,51)	CLOWN (0,51)
CAT (2,50)	TURKEY (0,51)	HARVEST (1,49)	PLANE (3,48)	GIRL (4,46)	STUDENT (1,50)	SCHOOL (2,50)	PAINTER (1,50)
THINKER (1,50)	READER (1,49)	LUNCH (3,48)	PALS (1,49)	WINNER (1,50)	KIDS (2,50)	LAB (2,50)	BUS (1,50)
PAINT (0,51)	ART (0,51)	ROCKER (4,47)	WRITER (1,51)	DANCER (1,50)	SLEEPER (2,50)	FOOTBALL (0,51)	BASKETBALL (1,51)

SKATES (6,46)	**BASEBALL** (1,49)	**SWIMMER** (6,51)	**KAYAK** (1,51)	**TENNIS** (2,50)	**VOLLEYBALL** (0,51)	**RUNNER** (7,44)	**POOL** (0,49)
GOLF (0,50)	**DONKEY** (0,51)	**ELEPHANT** (4,47)	**PANDA** (0,51)	**FROG** (1,50)	**OWL** (0,51)	**DOG** (2,50)	**RACCOON** (3,49)
ROOSTER (0,51)	**FISH** (1,49)	**FISH 2** (0,51)	**PEGASUS** (0,51)	**BUTTERFLY** (1,49)	**DINO** (1,49)	**DINO 2** (2,50)	**DINO 3** (2,49)
EAGLE (1,50)	**SPIDER*** (0,51)	**BEE*** (0,51)	**CRANE** (0,51)	**PHONE** (4,48)	**DRAMA** (0,51)	**MIME** (0,51)	**INDIAN** (4,51)
SPARTAN (0,51)	**VIKING** (0,51)	**MAIL** (0,51)	**MEMO** (1,50)	**PARK** (0,51)	**KNIGHT** (0,51)	**ROBOT** (3,49)	**MOON** (1,51)
UFO (1,50)	**RAIN** (0,51)	**ISLAND** (2,51)	**PLATE** (9,44)	**AIRES** (0,51)	**TAURUS** (4,44)	**GEMINI** (1,50)	**CANCER** (2,49)
LEO (0,51)	**VIRGO** (1,50)	**LIBRA** (5,46)	**SCORPIO** (0,50)	**SAGITTARIUS** (0,51)	**CAPRICORN** (0,51)	**AQUARIUS** (0,51)	**PISCES** (0,51)

*APPLE OWNERS ONLY! The 20 graphics indicated by the black outline are on side "B" of your Graphics Library disk.

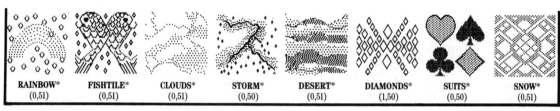

RAINBOW*	FISHTILE*	CLOUDS*	STORM*	DESERT*	DIAMONDS*	SUITS*	SNOW*
(0,51)	(0,51)	(0,51)	(0,50)	(0,51)	(1,50)	(0,50)	(0,51)

Works well as a Tile Pattern too!

Graphics Library 2

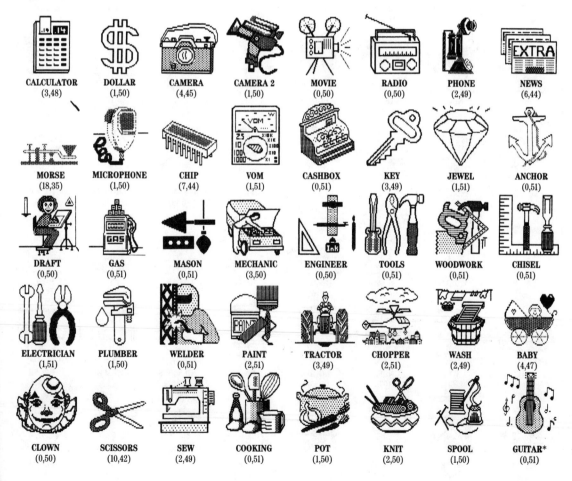

| CALCULATOR (3,48) | DOLLAR (1,50) | CAMERA (4,45) | CAMERA 2 (1,50) | MOVIE (0,50) | RADIO (0,50) | PHONE (2,49) | NEWS (6,44) |

| MORSE (18,35) | MICROPHONE (1,50) | CHIP (7,44) | VOM (1,51) | CASHBOX (0,51) | KEY (3,49) | JEWEL (1,51) | ANCHOR (0,51) |

| DRAFT (0,50) | GAS (0,51) | MASON (0,51) | MECHANIC (3,50) | ENGINEER (0,50) | TOOLS (0,51) | WOODWORK (0,51) | CHISEL (0,51) |

| ELECTRICIAN (1,51) | PLUMBER (1,50) | WELDER (0,51) | PAINT (2,51) | TRACTOR (3,49) | CHOPPER (2,51) | WASH (2,49) | BABY (4,47) |

| CLOWN (0,50) | SCISSORS (10,42) | SEW (2,49) | COOKING (0,51) | POT (1,50) | KNIT (2,50) | SPOOL (1,50) | GUITAR* (0,51) |

INSTRUMENTS (0,51)	**BAND*** (10,39)	**SCORE*** (2,49)	**KEYBOARD*** (3,48)	**JUKEBOX** (0,51)	**BINGO** (0,51)	**CHESS** (0,51)	**CAMP** (2,49)
BIKE (9,44)	**BALLOONS** (2,50)	**BOOTS** (1,50)	**CREST** (1,49)	**FOOL** (0,51)	**GEORGE** (1,50)	**ABE** (1,49)	**SHERLOCK** (0,51)
SIESTA (0,51)	**KING** (0,51)	**PHARAOH** (0,51)	**WEDDING** (0,51)	**JET** (2,48)	**SHIP** (7,43)	**SHIP 2** (1,49)	**PLANE** (3,47)
TRAIN (0,51)	**CABLE CAR** (1,51)	**CITY** (1,49)	**PARIS** (1,50)	**PISA** (1,50)	**WINDMILL** (3,49)	**LIBERTY** (5,46)	**TOTEM** (2,49)
MAP (3,47)	**WORLD** (4,45)	**STAMP** (0,51)	**BEACH** (0,51)	**SHELL** (1,50)	**DESERT*** (0,49)	**WISH** (0,51)	**MICROSCOPE** (1,50)
CHEM (0,51)	**RX** (1,51)	**NURSE** (0,51)	**DOCTOR** (0,51)	**DNA*** (0,51)	**GLASSES** (10,37)	**GET WELL** (1,51)	**BRUSH** (0,51)
CANDLE (0,51)	**TIME** (1,49)	**TORCH** (0,51)	**VANE** (1,50)	**BOWL** (1,51)	**SKI** (1,50)	**KARATE** (0,51)	**SCUBA** (0,51)

RACER	GOLF	SOCCER	FOOTBALL	GEESE	STAG	WHALE	CAT
(7,45)	(1,50)	(0,50)	(5,47)	(1,51)	(2,49)	(5,44)	(2,42)

FLAMINGO	CAMEL	SHEEP	KOALA	EASTER	SHAMROCK	JULY 4	CROSS
(0,50)	(1,49)	(11,41)	(0,51)	(1,49)	(1,50)	(3,48)	(0,51)

STAR	HANDS	CAROUSEL	CAMEO	GRAPES*	DRAGON	PLANTS	FISH*
(0,50)	(2,49)	(0,50)	(0,51)	(2,49)	(2,49)	(0,47)	(0,51)

Works well as a Tile Pattern too!

APPLE OWNERS ONLY! The 20 graphics indicated by the black outline are on side "B" of your Graphics Library disk.

Graphics Library 3

YIELD	STOP	LODGING	PAY PHONE	FOOD	UP	FRAGILE	KEEP DRY
(0,51)	(7,39)	(5,42)	(1,50)	(8,44)	(0,51)	(1,50)	(0,51)

MEN	WOMEN	WARNING	NO	NO SMOKING	FIRE	RECYCLE	WHICH WAY
(3,47)	(3,48)	(3,46)	(1,50)	(1,50)	(2,49)	(9,41)	(1,51)

QUIET	REMEMBER	SHAKE	CAUTION	TRUCE	LIFE BUOY	SECURITY	SOLAR
(0,51)	(0,51)	(9,42)	(3,49)	(2,48)	(5,46)	(0,44)	(0,51)

FAUCET (2,50) · RIGHT (12,39) · LEFT (13,40) · COMMUTE (0,51) · BUSY (4,47) · OFFICE (1,50) · MAIL (4,48) · TYPESETTER (2,49)

MEETING (3,48) · ARTIST (0,51) · CERTIFICATE (8,42) · FILE (2,49) · COFFEE (4,47) · RUSH (6,45) · TIRED (3,48) · BAR (0,51)

TAXI (13,39) · DANCE (0,51) · EXERCISE (6,46) · FAMILY (1,51) · WEIGHTS (1,51) · TEACHER (0,51) · FRESHMAN (0,51) · WHEELCHAIR (6,43)

CASE (0,51) · THUMBS UP (9,42) · THUMBS DOWN (11,37) · GAVEL (9,42) · MASTERCARD (11,40) · VISA (10,40) · REGISTER (9,41) · SAFE (7,44)

SALES (0,51) · MONEY (10,40) · DRIVER (5,46) · PUPPY (2,48) · PENGUIN (3,48) · BULBS (1,51) · SKI BEAR (4,46) · STAR (0,51)

NUTCRACKER (0,51) · WINDOW (1,50) · CHIMNEY (1,51) · HOHO (0,51) · LIGHTS (3,47) · KISS (0,46) · TREE TILE (1,51) · PARTRIDGE (0,51)

XMAS SONG (0,51) · CHUTE (0,51) · VAMPIRE (0,51) · LAMP (0,51) · MONKEY (1,51) · MERMAID (1,51) · CARPET (7,43) · GARGOYLE (0,51)

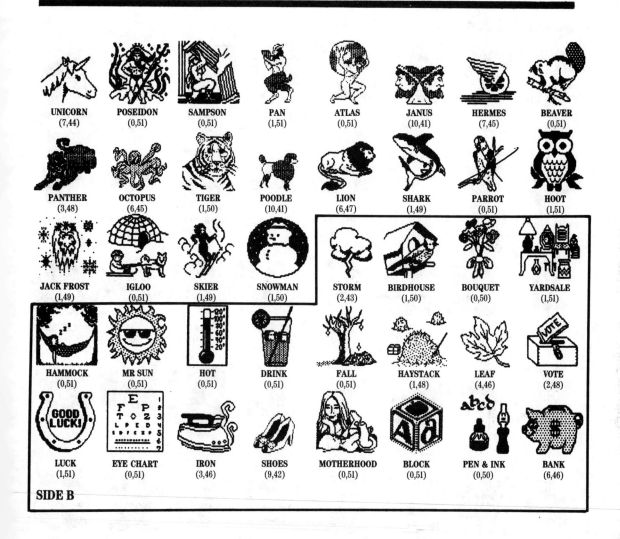

UNICORN (7,44)	POSEIDON (0,51)	SAMPSON (0,51)	PAN (1,51)	ATLAS (0,51)	JANUS (10,41)	HERMES (7,45)	BEAVER (0,51)
PANTHER (3,48)	OCTOPUS (6,45)	TIGER (1,50)	POODLE (10,41)	LION (6,47)	SHARK (1,49)	PARROT (0,51)	HOOT (1,51)
JACK FROST (1,49)	IGLOO (0,51)	SKIER (1,49)	SNOWMAN (1,50)	STORM (2,43)	BIRDHOUSE (1,50)	BOUQUET (0,50)	YARDSALE (1,51)
HAMMOCK (0,51)	MR SUN (0,51)	HOT (0,51)	DRINK (0,51)	FALL (0,51)	HAYSTACK (1,48)	LEAF (4,46)	VOTE (2,48)
LUCK (1,51)	EYE CHART (0,51)	IRON (3,46)	SHOES (9,42)	MOTHERHOOD (0,51)	BLOCK (0,51)	PEN & INK (0,50)	BANK (6,46)

SIDE B

*APPLE OWNERS ONLY! The 20 graphics indicated by the black outline are on side "B" of your Graphics Library disk.

Holiday Edition

JAN 1
(0,51)

NEW YEAR
(0,51)

NEW BEAR
(1,51)

KING
(3,51)

DRAGON 2
(0,47)

CHINESE NY*
(0,51)

SHADOW
(9,49)

MARDI GRAS
(0,51)

FOLK HEART
(0,51)

ROSEHEART
(3,50)

CUPID 2
(1,51)

HEARTS
(6,43)

LOVE CAT
(1,51)

LOVE BIRDS
(0,51)

VALENTINE
(11,41)

LINCOLN
(0,51)

GEORGE 2
(4,49)

GOLD
(0,51)

BEAR FOOL
(1,51)

KIDDER
(0,51)

PIE
(0,51)

PATRIOT
(0,51)

RABBIT
(0,51)

EASTER
(1,51)

LILY
(1,51)

BASKET
(3,48)

BUNNY 2
(0,50)

SECRETARY
(2,50)

ARBOR DAY
(4,49)

ROOTS
(0,51)

MAY 5
(1,51)

MOM DAY
(0,51)

MOM BEAR
(6,47)

MEMORIAL
(0,51)

FLAG DAY
(0,51)

DAD DAY
(1,51)

DAD BEAR
(2,49)

LIBERTY
(1,51)

UNCLE SAM
(0,51)

DECLARATION
(0,51)

EAGLE
(0,51)

GRANDPARENTS
(0,51)

COLUMBUS
(1,50)

BOSS
(6,51)

WEB
(0,51)

HAUNTING
(0,51)

WITCH 2
(0,51)

BOO
(0,51)

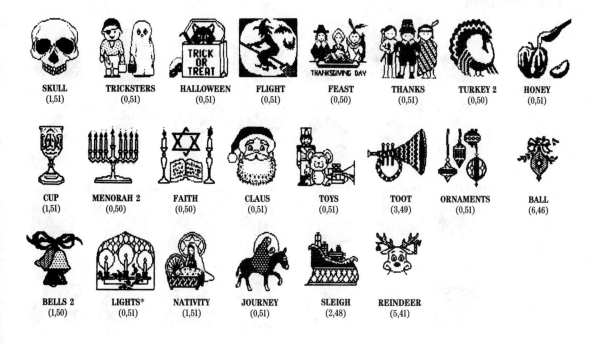

SKULL (1,51)	TRICKSTERS (0,51)	HALLOWEEN (0,51)	FLIGHT (0,51)	FEAST (0,50)	THANKS (0,51)	TURKEY 2 (0,50)	HONEY (0,51)
CUP (1,51)	MENORAH 2 (0,50)	FAITH (0,50)	CLAUS (0,51)	TOYS (0,51)	TOOT (3,49)	ORNAMENTS (0,51)	BALL (6,46)
BELLS 2 (1,50)	LIGHTS* (0,51)	NATIVITY (1,51)	JOURNEY (0,51)	SLEIGH (2,48)	REINDEER (5,41)		

Works well as a Tile Pattern too!

IBM Graphic Specifications

Program Disk

1 (4,48)　2 (5,47)　3 (3,45)　4 (5,46)　5 (5,47)　6 (1,51)　7 (0,47)

8 (3,47)　9 (5,50)　10 (4,48)　11 (1,50)　12 (3,49)　13 (0,51)　14 (6,46)

15 (5,44)　16 (4,48)　17 (1,51)　18 (0,50)　19 (2,49)　20 (2,50)　21 (1,50)

22 (3,48)　23 (18,40)　24 (2,50)　25 (1,50)　26 (1,51)　27 (5,46)　28 (8,43)

29 (8,44)　30 (1,49)　31 (2,50)　32 (4,46)　33 (5,46)　34 (2,50)　35 (1,50)

36 (1,50)　37 (1,48)　38 (4,48)　39 (1,51)　40 (5,47)　41 (1,51)　42 (5,45)

43 (2,50)　44 (2,47)　45 (4,45)　46 (2,49)　47 (1,49)　48 (10,41)　49 (5,46)

50 (6,44)　51 (4,47)　52 (3,46)　53 (4,47)　54 (0,50)　55 (3,49)　56 (1,48)

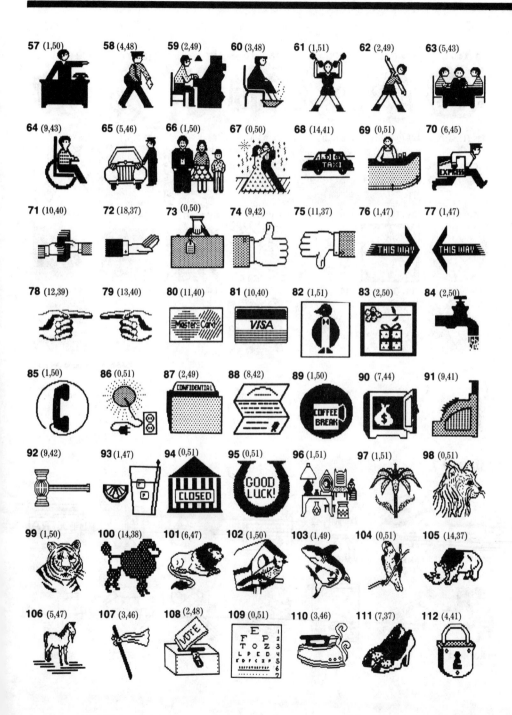

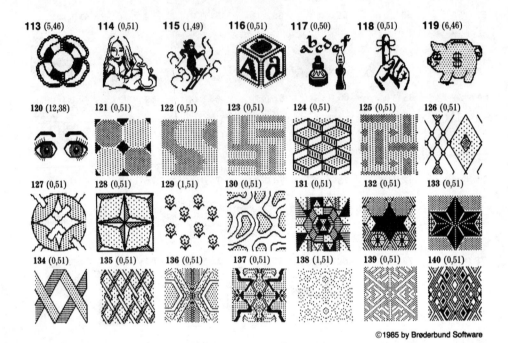

113 (5,46) **114** (0,51) **115** (1,49) **116** (0,51) **117** (0,50) **118** (0,51) **119** (6,46)

120 (12,38) **121** (0,51) **122** (0,51) **123** (0,51) **124** (0,51) **125** (0,51) **126** (0,51)

127 (0,51) **128** (0,51) **129** (1,51) **130** (0,51) **131** (0,51) **132** (0,51) **133** (0,51)

134 (0,51) **135** (0,51) **136** (0,51) **137** (0,51) **138** (1,51) **139** (0,51) **140** (0,51)

Graphics Library 1

DOLLAR (1,50) **CAMERA** (4,45) **CAMERA 2** (1,50) **MOVIE** (0,50) **RADIO** (0,50) **PHONE** (4,48) **PHONE2** (2,49) **NEWS** (6,44)

MORSE (18,35) **MICROPHONE** (1,50) **CHIP** (7,44) **VOM** (1,51) **CASHBOX** (0,51) **KEY** (3,49) **JEWEL** (1,51) **ANCHOR** (0,51)

DRAFT (0,50)	**GAS** (0,51)	**MASON** (0,51)	**MECHANIC** (3,50)	**ENGINEER** (0,50)	**TOOLS** (0,51)	**WOODWORK** (0,51)	**CHISEL** (0,51)
ELETRICIAN (1,51)	**PLUMBER** (1,50)	**WELDER** (0,51)	**PAINT2** (2,51)	**TRACTOR** (3,49)	**CHOPPER** (2,51)	**WASH** (2,49)	**BABY** (4,47)
DANCER (1,50)	**SLEEPER** (2,50)	**FOOTBALL** (0,51)	**TACKLE** (5,47)	**BASKETBALL** (1,51)	**SKATES** (6,46)	**BASEBALL** (1,49)	**SWIMMER** (6,51)
KAYAK (1,51)	**TENNIS** (2,50)	**VOLLEYBALL** (0,51)	**RUNNER** (7,44)	**POOL** (0,49)	**GOLF** (0,50)	**GOLF2** (1,50)	**BOWL** (1,51)
SKI (1,50)	**KARATE** (0,51)	**SCUBA** (0,51)	**RACER** (7,45)	**SOCCER** (0,50)	**DONKEY** (0,51)	**ELEPHANT** (4,47)	**PANDA** (0,51)
FIRE (0,51)	**ANGEL** (4,47)	**STOCKING** (1,50)	**CAROL** (1,50)				
MANAGER (4,47)	**RUDOLPH** (1,50)	**COOKIES** (2,49)	**TREE** (1,50)	**SNOWMAN** (2,49)	**SNOWGIRL** (0,51)	**HOME** (1,50)	**MAMA** (1,50)

JUNIOR
(0,50)

PAPA
(1,50)

DREIDEL
(1,50)

STAR
(0,50)

HANDS
(2,49)

CROSS
(0,51)

HOLLY
(1,51)

SANTA
(0,51)

SLED
(0,51)

CANE
(1,50)

NOEL
(0,51)

PARTY
(0,51)

PARTY2
(0,51)

GROUNDHOG
(2,51)

PATRICK
(0,51)

BUNNY
(0,51)

CHICK
(2,49)

EASTER
(1,49)

SHAMROCK
(1,50)

JULY4
(3,48)

FLOWERS
(0,51)

WEDDING
(0,51)

DUCK
(0,51)

FLAG
(1,50)

CHEF
(0,51)

PICNIC
(0,51)

CLOWN
(0,51)

CAT
(2,50)

TURKEY
(0,51)

HARVEST
(1,49)

PLANE
(3,48)

GIRL
(4,46)

STUDENT
(1,50)

SCHOOL
(2,50)

PAINTER
(1,50)

THINKER
(1,50)

READER
(1,49)

LUNCH
(3,48)

PALS
(1,49)

WINNER
(1,50)

KIDS
(2,50)

LAB
(2,50)

BUS
(1,50)

PAINT
(0,51)

ART
(0,51)

ROCKER
(4,47)

WRITER
(1,51)

CALCULATOR
(3,48)

FROG
(1,50)

OWL
(0,51)

DOG
(2,50)

RACCOON (3,49)	ROOSTER (0,51)	FISH (1,49)	FISH2 (0,51)	PEGASUS (0,51)	BUTTERFLY (1,49)	DINO (1,49)	DINO2 (2,50)
DINO3 (2,49)	EAGLE (1,50)	SPIDER (0,51)	BEE (0,51)	CRANE (0,51)	GEESE (0,51)	STAG (2,49)	WHALE (5,44)
CAT2 (2,42)	FLAMINGO (0,50)	CAMEL (1,49)	SHEEP (11,41)	KOALA (0,51)	DRAMA (0,51)	MIME (0,51)	INDIAN (4,51)
SPARTAN (0,51)	VIKING (0,51)	MAIL (0,51)	MEMO (1,50)	PARK (0,51)	KNIGHT (0,51)	ROBOT (3,49)	MOON (1,51)
UFO (1,50)	RAIN (0,51)	ISLAND (2,51)	PLATE (9,49)	AIRES (0,51)	TAURUS (4,44)	GEMINI (1,50)	CANCER (2,49)
LEO (0,51)	VIRGO (1,50)	LIBRA (5,46)	SCORPIO (0,50)	SAGITTARIUS (0,51)	CAPRICORN (0,51)	AQUARIUS (0,51)	PISCES (0,51)
RAINBOW (0,51)	FISTILE (0,51)	CLOUDS (0,51)	STORM (0,50)	DESERT (0,51)	DIAMONDS (1,50)	SUITS (0,50)	SNOW (0,51)

Graphics Library 2

(BRIDGE) (0,51)   CITY* (1,49)   (TOWN) (0,51)   (COUNTRY) (2,49)   (SCHOOL HOUSE) (0,51)   (CHURCH) (2,50)   PARIS (1,50)   PISA (1,50)

(MT FUJI) (0,51)   (CHINA) (2,51)   WINDMILL (3,49)   (ALOHA) (0,51)   LIBERTY (5,46)   (TEPEE) (5,49)   TOTEM (2,49)   WORLD (4,45)

STAMP (0,51)   BEACH* (0,51)   (SHORE) (0,51)   (BEACON) (0,51)   (SHELL) (1,50)   (DESERT) (0,49)   (WISH) (0,51)   (MICROSCOPE) (1,50)

CHEM (0,51)   RX (1,51)   NURSE (0,51)   DOCTOR (0,51)   (ATOM*) (0,51)   DNA* (0,51)   (GAS GRAPH*) (0,42)   (SAFETY PIN*) (0,51)

GET WELL (1,51)   BRUSH (0,51)   (BATH) (7,51)   CANDLE (0,51)   DRAGON (2,49)   UNICORN (7,44)   VAMPIRE (0,51)   (CREATURE) (1,51)

(MUMMY) (2,51)   (WITCH) (0,51)   (IMP) (1,49)   (FAIRY) (0,45)   (FROG PRINCE) (0,51)   LAMP (0,51)   MONKEYS (1,51)   MERMAID (1,51)

YIELD (0,51)   STOP (7,39)   LODGING (5,42)   FOOD (8,44)   UP (0,51)   FRAGILE (1,50)   KEEP DRY (0,51)   MEN (3,47)

WOMEN (3,48)	WARNING (3,46)	NO (1,50)	NO SMOKING (1,50)	FIRE (2,49)	RECYCLE (9,41)	WHICH WAY (1,51)	QUIET (0,51)
REMEMBER (0,51)	SHAKE (9,42)	CAUTION (3,49)	CLOWN (0,50)	(BOOKS) (5,51)	SCISSORS (10,42)	SEW (2,49)	COOKING (0,51)
POT (1,50)	KNIT (2,50)	SPOOL (1,50)	(MODEM) (1,50)	(PRINTER) (5,50)	GUITAR (0,51)	INSTRUMENTS (0,51)	BAND* (10,39)
SCORE* (2,49)	KEYBOARD* (3,48)	(SAX) (0,51)	JUKEBOX (0,51)	BINGO* (0,51)	CHESS (0,51)	CAMP (2,49)	(FISHING) (0,51)
BIKE (9,44)	BALLOONS* (2,50)	(BALLET) (0,51)	(SHOES*) (0,50)	BOOTS (1,50)	(COWBOY) (0,49)	CREST (1,49)	FOOL (0,51)
GEORGE (1,50)	ABE (1,49)	SHERLOCK (0,51)	SIESTA (0,51)	KING (0,51)	PHARAOH (0,51)	(GOLDEN) (0,51)	(SILVER) (0,51)
(BELLS) (0,51)	JET (2,48)	PLANE (3,47)	SHIP (7,43)	SHIP 2 (1,49)	(TUGBOAT) (2,39)	TRAIN (0,51)	CABLE CAR (1,51)

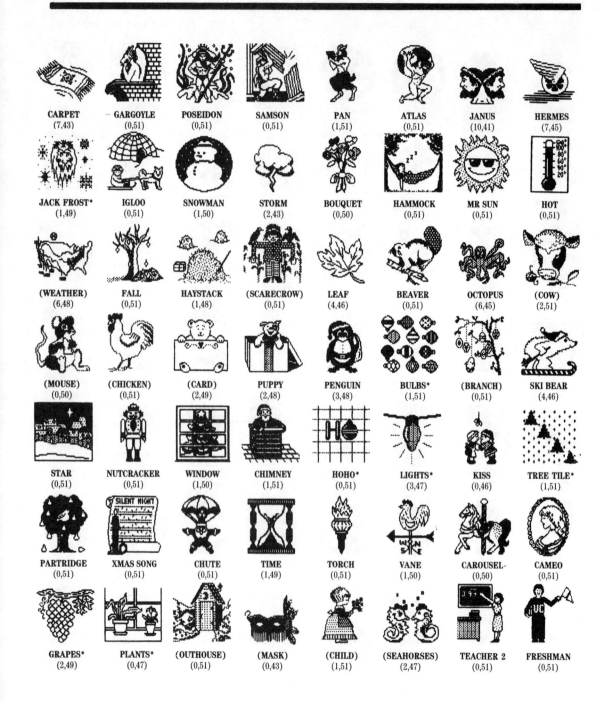

CARPET (7,43)	− GARGOYLE (0,51)	POSEIDON (0,51)	SAMSON (0,51)	PAN (1,51)	ATLAS (0,51)	JANUS (10,41)	HERMES (7,45)
JACK FROST* (1,49)	IGLOO (0,51)	SNOWMAN (1,50)	STORM (2,43)	BOUQUET (0,50)	HAMMOCK (0,51)	MR SUN (0,51)	HOT (0,51)
(WEATHER) (6,48)	FALL (0,51)	HAYSTACK (1,48)	(SCARECROW) (0,51)	LEAF (4,46)	BEAVER (0,51)	OCTOPUS (6,45)	(COW) (2,51)
(MOUSE) (0,50)	(CHICKEN) (0,51)	(CARD) (2,49)	PUPPY (2,48)	PENGUIN (3,48)	BULBS* (1,51)	(BRANCH) (0,51)	SKI BEAR (4,46)
STAR (0,51)	NUTCRACKER (0,51)	WINDOW (1,50)	CHIMNEY (1,51)	HOHO* (0,51)	LIGHTS* (3,47)	KISS (0,46)	TREE TILE* (1,51)
PARTRIDGE (0,51)	XMAS SONG (0,51)	CHUTE (0,51)	TIME (1,49)	TORCH (0,51)	VANE (1,50)	CAROUSEL· (0,50)	CAMEO (0,51)
GRAPES* (2,49)	PLANTS* (0,47)	(OUTHOUSE) (0,51)	(MASK) (0,43)	(CHILD) (1,51)	(SEAHORSES) (2,47)	TEACHER 2 (0,51)	FRESHMAN (0,51)

EXERCISE (6,46)	SALES (0,51)	COMMUTE (0,51)	COFFEE 2 (4,47)	(PIPES*) (0,51)	(LIPS) (11,38)	(BUBBLES) (1,50)

Holiday Edition

JAN1 (0,51)	NEW YEAR (0,51)	NEW BEAR (1,51)	KING (3,51)	DRAGON2 (0,47)	CHINESE NY* (0,51)	SHADOW (9,49)	MARDI GRAS (0,51)

FOLK HEART (0,51)	ROSEHEART (3,50)	CUPID2 (1,51)	HEARTS (6,43)	LOVE CAT (1,51)	LOVE BIRDS (0,51)	VALENTINE (11,41)	LINCOLN (0,51)

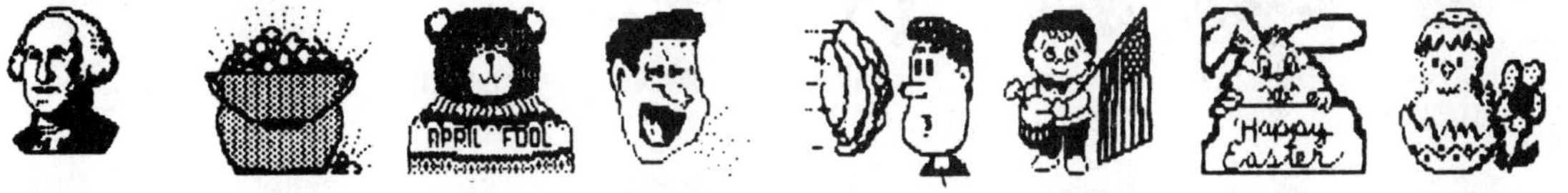

GEORGE2 (4,49)	GOLD (0,51)	BEAR FOOL (1,51)	KIDDER (0,51)	PIE (0,51)	PATRIOT (0,51)	RABBIT (0,51)	CHICK2 (0,51)

LILY (1,51)	BASKET (3,48)	(BUNNY3) (0,50)	SECRETARY (2,50)	ARBOR DAY (4,49)	ROOTS (0,51)	MAY 5 (1,51)	MOM DAY (0,51)

MOM BEAR (6,47)	MEMORIAL (0,51)	FLAG DAY (0,51)	DAD DAY (1,51)	DAD BEAR (2,49)	LIBERTY (1,51)	UNCLE SAM (0,51)	DECLARATION (0,51)

EAGLE (0,51)	GRANDPARENTS (0,51)	COLUMBUS (1,50)	BOSS (6,51)	WEB (0,51)	HAUNTING (0,51)	WITCH2 (0,51)	BOO (0,51)
SKULL (1,51)	TRICKSTERS (0,51)	HALLOWEEN (0,51)	FLIGHT (0,51)	FEAST (0,50)	THANKS (0,51)	(TURKEY2) (TURKEY3) (0,50)	HONEY (0,51)
CUP (1,51)	MENORAH2 (0,50)	FAITH (0,50)	CLAUS (0,51)	TOYS (0,51)	TOOT (3,49)	ORNAMENTS (0,51)	BALL (6,46)
BELLS2 (1,50)	(CANDLE2) (0,51)	NATIVITY (1,51)	JOURNEY (0,51)	SLEIGH (2,48)	REINDEER (5,41)		

Works well as a Tile Pattern too!

About the Art Grid

If you can't find a graphic that fits your design why not draw your own! The art grid is the tool to use when you want to create an original graphic. Just copy the grid on a copying machine, grab a pencil, and you're ready to go!

Like graph paper, the art grid has many small boxes. Each box represents the position of a dot in the Graphic Editor drawing surface. Fill in the boxes on the art grid. When your drawing is exactly the way you want it, fill in the dots in the Graphic Editor in the exact same positions. Every tenth box on the art grid is highlighted for you to make it easier to identify its position. The position of every dot in the Graphic Editor is labeled on screen.

Copy your art grid drawing onto the Graphic Editor drawing surface and you'll have a new piece of art at your command! Save it to use or modify as often as you'd like.

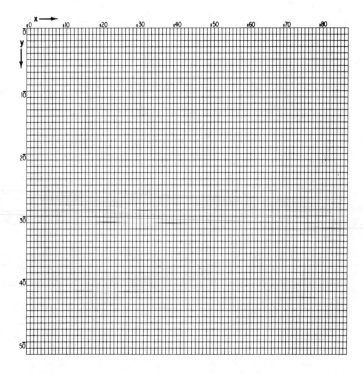

Brøderbund Presents Four More Ways To Be Creative With Your Computer

In addition to **The Print Shop** series of programs, Brøderbund offers a variety of other products that will stimulate your creativity. They let you draw, paint, design, animate, and even build toys!

ANIMATE PACKAGE

With **Animate** you can add realistic movement to your drawings and designs. In fact, you'll actually be working with the same sophisticated tool used by Brøderbund designers to create award-winning graphics. The lifelike characters and backgrounds you create can be made into cartoons, movies and show disks. Includes pre–drawn objects and backgrounds.

DAZZLE DRAW PACKAGE

This double-high-resolution paint program unlocks the power, color, and detail of the Apple IIc and 128K Apple IIe. It's simple enough for beginners, yet sophisticated enough to produce professional-quality graphics, prints and slides. Features pull-down menus and windows. You'll work with a 16-color palette; dozens of patterns, brush shapes and sizes, and many other options.

FANTAVISION PACKAGE

With **Fantavision,** even beginners can produce animated TV-style cartoons and "movies." You'll see your drawings come alive as they turn, run, fly...following your every command. Animation happens instantly, because **Fantavision** does so much of the work for you. With special tools called "tweening" and "transforming," **Fantavision** draws up to 64 "in-between" drawings for every one you draw!

THE TOY SHOP PACKAGE

Make your own toys! This award-winning program lets you build a steam engine, an antique carousel...a total of 20 marvelous mechanical models that really work. Choose a project from the on-screen menu, customize it and print. Then cut out and assemble the model. Adhesive-backed cardboard and other supplies are included (You can use the program over and over – so go ahead and make as many copies of each toy as you want.)

To order any of these programs, or to learn more about our products, contact your local Brøderbund Software dealer or call Brøderbund at (415) 492-3200.